ỊCHỤAJA
in Igbo Traditional Religion:

A Comparative Study with SACRIFICE
in Judaism, Hinduism and Christianity

Chika Okpalike

iUniverse, Inc.
New York   Bloomington

ỊCHỤAJA in Igbo Traditional Religion:

A Comparative Study with SACRIFICE in Judaism, Hinduism and Christianity

iUniverse books may be ordered through booksellers or by contacting:

iUniverse
1663 Liberty Drive
Bloomington, IN 47403
www.iuniverse.com
1-800-Authors (1-800-288-4677)

Because of the dynamic nature of the Internet, any Web addresses or links contained in this book may have changed since publication and may no longer be valid. The views expressed in this work are solely those of the author and do not necessarily reflect the views of the publisher, and the publisher hereby disclaims any responsibility for them.

ISBN: 978-0-595-53211-7 (pbk)
ISBN: 978-0-595-63270-1 (ebk)

Printed in the United States of America

iUniverse rev. date: 12/17/2008

Dedication

To all who have struggled to restore and preserve the waning
culture and religion of the tribal peoples of Africa

Acknowledgement

I thank God for being God ever and always and for giving me the graces to acknowledge this fact of His being. I appreciate my supervisor in the course of studying Master of Arts (MA) in Religion, Rev. Fr. Prof. Anthony N. O. Ekwunife, under whose tutelage I have learnt and developed this academic work. I thank him especially for his meticulousness in reading the work and insistence on what must be done and for offering to write the forward to this work, which he, without reservation found expedient to be published for academic purposes. I am grateful to my bishop, Most Rev. S. A. Okafor, together with his Auxiliary, Most Rev. P. C. Ezeokafor, for granting the permission to do this study. I thank my colleagues—Rev. Frs. Vincent Ifeme, Gregory Adibe, and Charles Umeoji—for their numerous offers of assistance and support in the course of my study. I also thank Rev. Fr. Raymond Arazu for always opening his door whenever I needed to talk with him. I thank my big brother, Dr. Nnaemeka Martin Okpalike, for his unmitigated encouragement and for always easing my way through financial hurdles and his wife, Uju Cynthia Okpalike, for being exceptionally supportive.

Forward

Studies in African Traditional Religion (ATR) in their various ramifications are advancing towards a more perfect stage in terms of deeper insights and analysis of elements of that religion. Facilitators in this upward thrust come not only from the insights of past scholars on this subject but also from a cultural-area approach and interpretative tools of allied studies like theology, anthropology, sociology, philosophy, and linguistics.

In light of the above, the present book on Sacrifice in Igbo Traditional Religion (ITR), aptly titled *Ịchụaja*, finds its rightful place. With what looks like a heart-warming academic throb, the author of this book revisited the usual claims of previous scholars on Sacrifice in ITR. Dissatisfied with the nomenclature *Aja* in transliterating the English *Sacrifice* for what he regarded as the heart of ITR, he swiftly moved towards a reconstruction with the Igbo word *Ịchụaja* as a strong hinge. As he succinctly quips in the introductory section:

> The aim of this work is to reassess the etymological
> formulation of *Ịchụaja* by evaluating its status

among all other ritual elements and exploring what constitutes it as a practical action in ITR.

To achieve the above gigantic task, the author made use of what is often regarded as polymorphic method or interdisciplinary method with anthropo-religious, comparative, historico-philological, and theological approaches in the forefront. Finally, with further analysis of the various nuances of *Ịchụaja*, he landed on curious conclusions which readers will find fascinating and provocative.

Thus, he conclusively snipped with academic assurance (2008:161-2):

> We believe that the whole idea of sacrifice in ITR has been radicalized and made more profound and meaningful. Before this work, *Ịchụaja* has been viewed from a negative perspective; the work has opened further vistas to the understanding of what the votaries of ITR do in a more positive light.

Even if readers of the contents of this work disagree on some issues raised by its author, they cannot but appreciate the courage and innovative trends of the writer. Like a good architect, he pulls down the old edifice of this practical element of ITR only to build with alacrity what looked like a lost ground. Therein is the genius of this work.

While passing kudos on the efforts of the author, I warmly recommend the work to all especially genuine readers of ATR/ITR.

Rev. Fr. Prof. A. Ekwunife
Department of Religion,
University of Nigeria, Nsukka.
March 17, 2008.

Preface

The first version of this work, which began under the title *Ịchụaja: The Heart of Practical Igbo Traditional Religion*, was submitted to the Department of Religion, University of Nigeria, Nsukka for the award of a Master of Arts Degree (MA) in Religion (African Traditional Religion). Under the present title and form, we tried to improve on it and to incorporate other relevant topics into this discourse. Rendering the word *sacrifice* in Igbo, on the one hand, and transliterating the word *Ịchụaja* in English, on the other hand, is a matter of great concern to the present writer. This concern seems to have been taken for granted by scholars who have done extensive studies in the topic of sacrifice in Igbo Traditional Religion (ITR). It does seem a general consensus—and we agree too—that *Aja* is the generic name for sacrifice in ITR. But *Ịchụaja* is a verb form (infinitive) that has not enjoyed this generic application at the hands of scholars. Nevertheless, the present writer found out that *Ịchụaja* is a ritual action performed at one point in all varieties of ritual acts in ITR. If *Ịchụ* means 'to drive away,' as Basden (1966), Arinze (1970), Metuh (1985), and Umeh (1997) averred, then what is *Aja*?

These scholars must end up saying "*Aja* is evil" if they will be consistent with their interpretation. Curious!

The Igbo Catechism of the Catholic Church underscores *Aja* as an offering due to God alone for the living and the dead. The Owerri Catholic Province's version of the document precisely said '*Aja bụ iji* 'victim....' ('*Aja* is offering a victim'). However, we are of the opinion in this work that *Ịchụaja* is the heart of ITR. Therefore, once the concept is missed, it will be difficult to come to terms with any idea in the religion. We choose then to investigate what *Aja* is and what the transliteration of the word *Ịchụ* should be in ITR. The purpose is to set a comprehensible footing for ITR because *Ịchụaja* is at the heart of its religious expression.

Ịchụaja is evidently a practice at the heart of Igbo Traditional Religion (ITR). It is pertinent, therefore, to study the phenomenon and found a theory upon which to ground the concept, believing that a proper understanding of the concept will throw more light on the ideas hidden in ITR. *Ịchụaja* has always been seen—and correctly too—as an element alongside others in ITR. It is the conviction of the present writer that it is not just an element, but an element that lends meaning to all other elements. The problem this work has highlighted is that *Ịchụaja* has been seriously misconstrued by a number of scholars. If this is true, as we think, it is then worth the labour to study this phenomenon further. Alongside this misconstrual, *Ịchụaja* or *Aja* has been understood either as sacrifice or as an element in the sacrificial system of ITR.

Further, one of the major concerns of this work is that the theories of sacrifice that have been advanced by a number of Western scholars were motivated by their Christian background, and Christianity itself has inculcated the world with its idea of sacrifice for centuries. It has laboured the word—sacrifice—so much with the singular idea of Christ's death that sacrifice can only be about Christianity. However, the concept of sacrifice from its origins *sacer facere* is very close to that of *Ịchụaja*, and unless a theory on which *Ịchụaja* could be adequately grounded is found either within or outside existing theories, we still leave an open area for the misconstrual of the whole of ITR. ITR should not appear bizarre and barbaric; it is a religion with a philosophy that can be at the same time comprehensible and systematic.

This work attempts to verify which of the ideas mentioned above could suffice for a proper understanding of *Ịchụaja*—sacrifice proper or an element in the sacrificial system—and focuses on eliminating certain arbitrary interpretations that have so far been imposed on ITR. We adopted the participant-observer method: coming empty-handed to the area of ITR, allowing its elements to inform us, and interpreting its data from within. *Ịchụaja* has been observed in this work to be one consistent element in all practical activities of ITR. It is fairly difficult to isolate it as an element having a kind of independence from all other elements. *Ịchụaja* is precisely the ritual slaying of a victim, an act which consecrates and sanctifies the victim and the sacrificer. *Ịchụaja* is a fundamentum, what it connotes is varied—gift to the deity, homage to the deity, expiation, communion with the deity, life transmitted to the deity and, subsequently, conferred upon the sacrificer, and so forth. Nevertheless, the present writer thinks that these connotations are founded upon the contemporary understanding of the word informed by the Christian concept of sacrifice.

Africans are reputed to be notoriously religious. Indeed, religious ideas that have permeated the world were generated in Africa, yet for whatever reason, the Traditional Religion of Africa is struggling to avoid extinction. The overpowering Western criterion has ideologically impoverished everything African, including Africans' religious pride. The danger escalates when Africans themselves join in offering more weapons for further destruction, no matter how negligible. The extinction of a race begins with insensitivity to the possibility of its extinction by those who should know. The element of *Ịchụaja* in ITR can be presented in a positive light when we employ patience and sympathy to observe its dynamics. Continued effort to present the African lot in a bad light must be fought with the same force with which it corrodes the African pride. If we have lost the trend, we should acknowledge our faults: not make up things for which Africa will continually be regarded as savage and dark. Our religion should be logical and philosophical in as much as it is rife with the mystical and practical. We sincerely attempt to pull off the garb of our religious and philosophical bias and thread the grounds of ITR with the element - *Ịchụaja*.

Chika J. B. G. Okpalike
Department of Religion,
Nnamdi Azikiwe University, Awka,
Nigeria
July 18, 2008

Contents

List of Tables

List of Figures

Abbreviations

ANE   Ancient Near East

APA   American Psychological Association

ATR   African Traditional Religion

CCC   The Catechism of the Catholic Church

ITR   Igbo Traditional Religion

SC   Sacrosactum Concilium

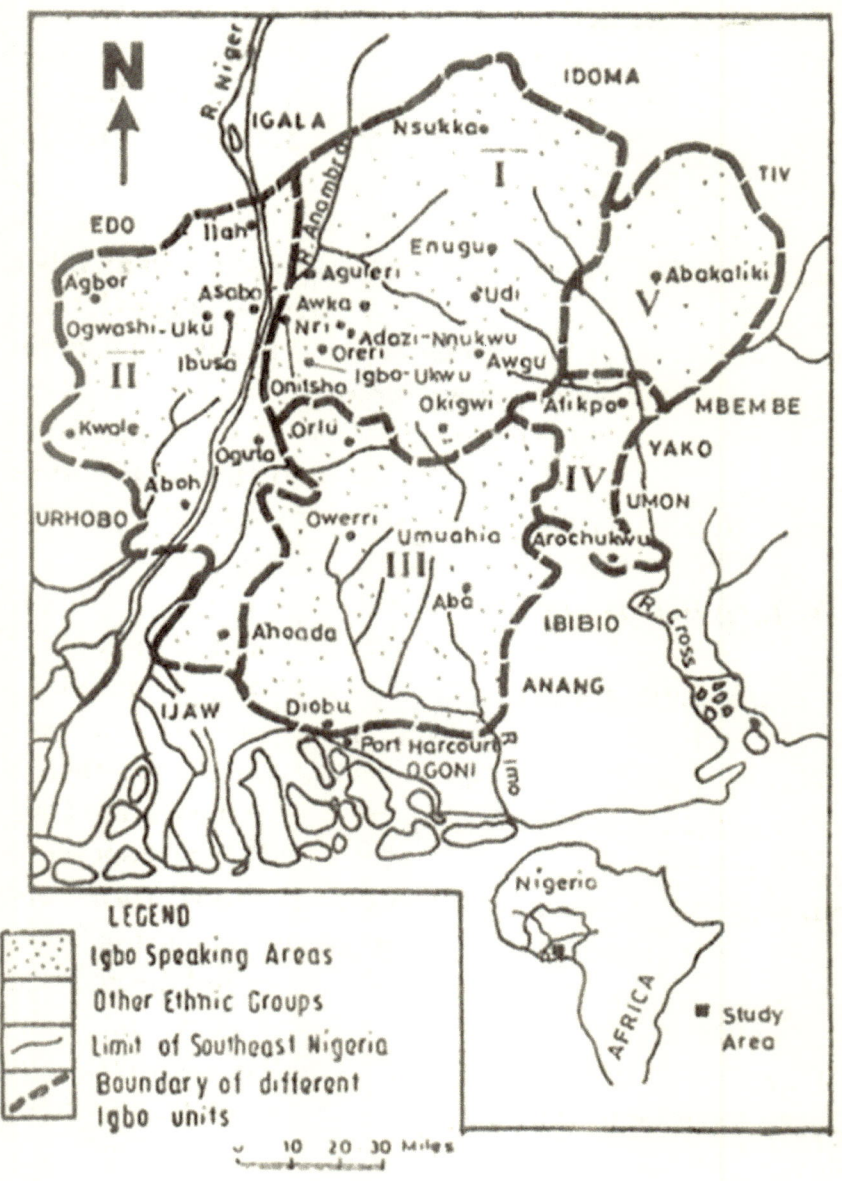

Figure 1. Map of South-East Nigeria showing Igbo settlements.

Introduction

Background, Aim, and Scope

Religion is as old as humankind, yet it is not easy to find an all-embracing definition for it. Scholars who have attempted to define it end up with formulations that are either too inclusive or too exclusive. In general, we know that there are theistic religions, such as Hinduism and Christianity, and nontheistic religions, such as Buddhism. Theistic religion has to do with humankind's acknowledgement of both the existence of a supernatural being and the influence of this being upon the world. The varieties of theistic religions spring from various conceptions of the nature of this supernatural being, the manner of his relationship with man, and the mode of maintaining this relationship on the part of man.

Igbo Traditional Religion (ITR) acknowledges this supernatural being as an entity popularly referred to as *Chukwu* (the Supreme God) and variously understood as *Obinigwe*, *Ezechitokeabịama*, *Olisa*, *Osebulụwa* and so forth. The Igbo—the sole votaries of ITR—also aver that the physical world was created (directly or indirectly) by or emanated from him. In the language of Aristotle, he is the uncaused cause of the physical world. The theory of this causation is not uniform, nor does this fact concern us in the present work. However, this being is not the sole object of ITR. Together with him, though in the lower sphere of spiritual hierarchy, are *Ụmụmmụọ* (pure spirits), *Arụsị* (localized spirits), and *Ndịichie* (disembodied spirits). Remarkably, these spirits can be both benevolent and malevolent; they are not programmed with a steady nature. Because man is the ontological centre of the Igbo universe and these spirits exist for his welfare, they react to man in accordance with his moral and ritual state. In the Igbo world, morality is interiorly tied to religion. The Igbo always seek harmony with nature around them and with these spirits, in order to live in peace in a world of vagaries and vicissitudes. *Ịchụaja* has been identified as the heart of ITR and the singular means through which the Igbo in ITR achieve this harmony. *Ịchụaja* constitutes that precise moment when the achievement of this harmony is ritualized.

It is pertinent to mention here that Christianity dominated the world for centuries and during those years set the program and criteria by which concepts and the nature of the world may be understood and interpreted. ITR, during the colonial period, received its own share of this domineering influence, which produced *Aja* as an acceptable transliteration of sacrifice. But for the expediency of accretion in cultural interaction, especially in this epoch of globalization, the present writer would have said, "Let *Aja* alone and be gone with sacrifice." Nevertheless, we accept this product of the missionaries—*Aja*—to be understood as 'sacrifice.' Against this backdrop *Ịchụaja* as a process in sacrifice needs a proper conceptualization. As the soul of ITR, a misconception is a mortal danger.

The aim of this work is to reassess the etymological formulation of *Ịchụaja* by evaluating its status among all other ritual elements and exploring what constitutes it as a practical action in ITR. It is an expository exercise to locate *Ịchụaja* within the boundaries of other ritual elements in ITR. From the onset, we have not been in agreement with what we consider the verdict of earlier researchers, namely that the word *Ịchụaja* is composed of two Igbo words *Ịchụ*, meaning 'to drive away,' and *Aja*, meaning 'evil' or something similar. Apart from examining the occasions of *Ịchụaja* in the ritual practices of ITR, understanding the component words that make it up will give us clues to the theoretical foundation of the practice as seen in ITR. Scholars are more often interested in the utilitarian or pragmatic value of sacrifice, but our aim is to establish a metaphysical foundation of *Ịchụaja* upon which praxis or utility may be built. Moreover, the idea of 'driving away' has not given us enough insight into the theory of sacrifice on which to ground *Ịchụaja* as a practice in ITR.

We also aim at founding a veritable theory of sacrifice that could adequately interpret the idea of *Ịchụaja* in ITR. We shall reduce the word *Ịchụaja* to a singular action that will become the common denominator of the ritual in all instances and by which it shall be henceforth identified. We shall also seek to comprehend how *Ịchụaja* would and would not at the same time adequately translate as 'sacrifice.' The topic of the research, *Ịchụaja: The Heart of Practical Igbo Traditional Religion*, which gave rise to this work, already informs us that this work should establish ITR as practical and place *Ịchụaja* at the heart or center of its expression. Further, this work aims at a face-lift for ITR in the sense that this element of the religion—*Ịchụaja*—has been misconstrued, thereby continuing the tradition initiated by earlier Western anthropologists, explorers, and missionaries and downgrading the religion.

The Igbo are the present occupants of the Southeastern territories of Nigeria. Some scholars who have researched the origins of this race have given it a common ancestory with the Efik, Ibibio, and Kalabari of South-South Nigeria (Abasika, 1993; Ogbukagu, 2001), insinuating that they all are of a Jewish stock. The geographical boundaries of the Igbo show the Igala, Idoma, and Tiv on the northern borders; the Ijaw and Ogoni on the southern borders; the Ibibio, Anang, Yako, and Mbembe on the east; and the Edo and Urhobo on the west. To make for balanced research, we shall define locations for the northern, north-central, south-central, inland-eastern, southern, and western parts of the Igbo country. Beyond cultural species and religious specifications, we shall also investigate dialectical differences in phonology and morphology of the various parts of the country to help fine-tune our findings.

Problem, Significance, and Method

Arinze (1970), Basden (1966), Metuh (1985), and Umeh (1997) are some of the scholars who have done extensive work on the theme of *Aja* and *Ịchụaja*. They are all agreed that the word *Ịchụaja* is made up of two Igbo words— *Ịchụ* and *Aja*—, and in this, the present witer is in agreement with them. Amazingly, none of them minced words in stating that *Ịchụ* means 'drive away' (Arinze, 1970, p. 61; Basden, 1966, p. 57; Metuh, 1985, p. 60; Umeh, 1997, p. 90), but all had difficulty stating categorically what *Aja* is within the same composition, leaving their readers with the option of presuming its meaning. While Basden transliterated 'drive away evil,' Arinze rendered 'drive away sacrifice,' Metuh indicated 'drive away evil spirits,' and Umeh wrote 'drive away *Aja*.' In all these renderings, "what is *Aja*?" Most readers seem to rest content with the statement "a sacrifice to ward off evil spirits," used by all of them to describe *Ịchụaja*, presuming that it is a necessary implication of *Ịchụ*. Such readers are not agitated by the thought that *Aja* is predicated upon the infinitive form *Ịchụ* and should, as an object, be a noun. If we take *evil* (Basden), *sacrifice* (Arinze), *evil spirits* (Metuh), or *Aja* (Umeh) to be the predicate of the verb *Ịchụ* in the composition *Ịchụaja*, we shall be incurring a good deal of confusion and contradiction.

On the other hand, Ifesieh (1989, pp. 240-241) carefully avoided this mix-up in his list of kinds of *Aja*. For instance, he understood *Aja alọ* as a kind of *Aja* done in *Ịkpụalọ*. The precise action performed for the ritual act to deserve the name *Aja alọ* must be contained in the verb *Ịchụ*, as Metuh (1985, p. 60) averred. Ifesieh did not find it expedient to investigate '*Ịchụ*' further, yet it is this search that bothers us in this work because, avoiding the confusion will not solve the problem since *Ịchụaja* is a concept both in demotic and contemporary Igbo. Further curiousity arises with the definition of *Aja* given by Nwosu and Otteh (1996) who revised and Edited the Onitsha version of the Igbo mini catechism of the Catholic Church: "*Aja bụ ihe a na-ehunyere sọ Chukwu site n'aka Ụkọchukwu, n'ihi na Chukwu bụ Dinwenụ na Osebrụwa nke ihe nile.*" (Aja is *something* (*ihe*) offered-up to God alone through the hands of a priest, because God is Lord and the bearer/sustainer of all things.) That "something," which this Onitsha Province version of the document failed to mention specifically, the Owerri Province version rendered as "*Aja bụ iji 'victim' huoro Chineke site n'aka priest.*" (*Aja* is the offering of a victim to God through the hands of a priest.) This rendering suggests that, outside the generic concept of *Aja* as sacrifice, there may be another nuance to the concept that has been unaddressed. *Ịchụaja*, as interpreted by the scholars mentioned above, may have been hurriedly done; it sounds odd that a handful of researchers in ITR are part of the theology represented in the work of Nwosu and Otteh. Furthermore, Nwosu and Otteh (1996) wrote, "*Mass dị asọ bụ aja ahụ na ọbara nke Dinwenụ anyi Jeesu Kristi ehunyeere Chukwu site n'aka ụkọchukwu maka ndi di ndụ na ndi nwụrụ anwụ.*" (The Holy Mass is the sacrifice of the Body and Blood of our Lord Jesus Christ offered to God through the instrumentality of a priest both for the living and the dead.) This statment indicates that Mass is a kind of *Aja*. When we say '*Ichụaja Mass,*' which we normally do, what do we mean? 'Driving away the sacrifice of the Mass?' If we do not succeed in achieving a veritable conceptualization of the meaning of *Ichụ* and *Aja*, then we should, at least, be disturbed by this confusion. The present writer thinks that it is from within the framework of the conceptual analysis of *Ichụaja* that this illusive meaning can be elicited.

This study is significant for various reasons. It could shed light on the stage of ATR from an African participant observer. Great efforts have already been put in by a number of scholars in this perspective—Arinze (1970), Basden (1966) Ifesieh (1989), Ekwunife (1990), Umeh (1997), Ogbukagu (1997), and Arazu (2005), to mention just a few. Yet the work strives to throw further light on *Ichụaja*, taking it for granted that, unless its concept and religious significance are made clear, the very center of ITR has been eroded. When *Ichụaja* has been adequately conceptualized, ITR could then be studied and understood systematically like all other world religions. The research acknowledges that, in as much as the Igbo—unlike the Jew and the Christian—did not proselytize their religion, it is not bereft of all universal character. The concept of *Ichụaja* will, it is hoped, break the nationalistic, obsolete, and localized barriers of ITR and open the religion up to a more comprehensive, universal application. The study also signifies the dynamism and prolificacy of ITR that it could survive the heartless arsenal and mutiny heaved upon it by Europe and Christianity. It should, therefore, seek the possibility of giving a more profound understanding of this element, which the writer considers a serious lack in some works bordering on this same theme.

In order to achieve our goals as stipulated, we must heed Idowu (1973), who had warned against two categories of researchers who must be avoided in the study of religion: "the traveler who takes back among other things, reports on religions of the foreign countries of his travels, and the stay-at-home investigator who waits eagerly at the other end for the supply of information of which the traveler is always full to over-flowing" (p. 6). Further, Ekwunife(1999) divided the researchers into religious phenomena into four classes.

[1.]   Curious seekers.
[2.]   Stake seekers.
[3.]   Serious searchers.
[4.]   Open-minded searchers. (p. 17-19).

Recommending the fourth group of searchers with a new methodology, he called this new approach participated observer method. Scholars are of the opinion that this method is more plausible in the study of alien beliefs and practices.

In a more technical manner, this work will source data from extensive library work, oral interviews, and observations of the very situations and circumstances of *Ịchụaja*. Interpretation of collected data will be both comparative and analytic, without down-playing participation and observation. In our comparative analysis, the Christian idea and its ally—Judaism—will feature prominently. However, even while being a comparative study, this work is expository in locating *Ịchụaja* within the other elements of ITR. We shall avoid coming to the verdict of our search through established theories, especially those outside the boundaries of ATR. We desire to plunge into *Ịchụaja* as it presents itself practically in ITR. Finally, to allow for a free, unobstructed reading, APA (American Psychological Association) method of reference will be employed.

Definition of Terms

Sacrifice. Though we seem to be left with no options, we are wary of equating the word *sacrifice* with *Ịchụaja* from the onset to avoid unnecessary confusion in the system of setting up our data. It is pertinent to form a definition of *sacrifice*, so that when we do use the term, it will be clear what we imply. On the one hand, we shall adopt the idea of Daly (1999) concerning sacrifice as that which "stands at the center of a dynamic process in which the divine (or spiritual) and the human come into contact" (p. 923). Sacrifice is a ritual action in any religion that is capable of opening up the spiritual terrain for the human performer of such an action. It is a ritual medium through which the closed-up spiritual world opens itself to human seekers to behold and interpret to their benefit. On the other hand, we take also the idea of Nola (1973, quoted in Daly (1999): "Sacrifices and offerings are alienations of human goods by way of destruction (sacrifice) or simple renunciation (offering) vis-à-vis the (invisible) power(s), according to purposes and in function of deeds or concern which differ from culture to culture" (p. 923). While Daly brought out the mediatory nature of sacrifice, Nola emphasized the proper action that constitutes sacrifice namely "by way of destruction ... or simple denunciation." Nola also incorporated the secularized idea of sacrifice in his definition.

Furthermore, it is pertinent to mention that two nuances could be deciphered in the etymological presentation of the word *sacrifice*.

1. From Latin *sacrum*—'holy'—and *facere*—'to make, do, or perform'; thus, it would imply 'performing a holy act.' This definition is more philosophical or abstract in presentation. Granted that every sacrifice is a holy act, this definition seems to swallow the practical and mystical aspect of sacrifice. However, 'to do or perform a holy act' should be understood in this context that a place, thing, or person is set apart for and consecrated to a divine personage. As underscored in Suarez (1990):

> The word sacrifice—from *sacrum facere*, to do something holy—meant that a person or a thing was consecrated to the divinity, made sacred and withdrawn from ordinary use if it was a thing, or dedicated to the service of the god if it is a person. (p. 28)

2. From Latin *sacer*—'holy' and—*ficere (interficere)*—'to slay or kill,' it would imply 'to slay a holy (separated) thing' or 'holy slaying.' This definition brings out succinctly the practical and mystical aspect of the term. Though it is implied in the first instance, this implication can only be known to a few who may know deeper than mere words can reveal. *Ficere* is derived from *interficere*. It also brings out a very important aspect of sacrifice—immolation

Ichuaja: The word *Ichuaja* shall be seen as adequately translating sacrifice; therefore, there might not be any further stress in defining *Ichuaja*. The whole work could also be viewed as an extensive effort to verify this adequacy of *Ichuaja* as a proper translation of *sacrifice*. For the purpose of this study, *Ichuaja* should be understood as a ritual paying of ransom by votaries to the gods and spirits of their religion in order to gain the favours of the latter (*Do ut des*). This ransom is a victim, which must suffer an ignominious treatment, debasing to its nature to signify the total submission of the votary to the surpassing power of the gods and spirits. Such abasement will be expected to yield contentment for the gods and spirits and, in turn, well-being and favours from them to the votaries who may or may not (depending on the circumstance) partake of the sacred meal consequent to the ritual of *Ịchụaja*.

Practical: By *practical* is meant that which we experience but which at the same time shadows the real things which are the mainstay of the religion.

Heart: By *heart* is meant core, nucleus, or fulcrum. It conveys the image of that around which the whole practice of the religion revolves and the idea that, once it is dispensed with, the whole edifice of the religion would collapse, but with it, the idea of the religion could be perfectly understood. For instance, Christianity is built upon the idea that "Jesus is Lord." Christian doctrines are judged true or false by the fact of contradiction to or conformity with this basic statement. Once this mark is missed, Christians can go berserk in the interpretations of their Holy Writ without making any correct statement.

Ritual elements: By *ritual elements* we mean those practical actions performed within the cult of ITR worship. Evidently these rituals are endless. We shall make effort to categorize them into four major elements: *Imedommụọ, Ịgọmmụọ, Ịrọmmụọ,* and *Irummụọ*. Individual communities have peculiar names and features for theirs, which, however, must fall within our four categories. We may see local variables in *Ịkpụarụ, Ịkwụala, Ịtụjụala, Ikeji, Imoọka, Imengụma, Iruchi, Itụegbo, Iruajana, Ịtụarụsị, Ịkwaiyi, Ịgbanjahụ,*

Ịdọajaezelu, Imeogovu, Ịsaifi, Ịrụagwụ, Iruọfọ, Ịraụgọ, Ịtaatụ, Ihejịọkụ, Ịguar, and so forth. These ritual elements are the hallmark of ITR worship while *Ịchụaja* is the highpoint of each and every one of them.

Igbo Traditional Religion: Ekwunife (1990) gave a profound and enduring definition of ITR:

> Igbo traditional religion means those living institutionalized religious beliefs and practices which are rooted in the past Igbo religious culture; a religion that was transmitted to the present overt and covert votaries by successive Igbo fore bears mainly through oral traditions (myths, folktales, songs and dances, liturgies, rituals, proverbs, pithy sayings and names), sacred institutions like sacred specialists and persons, initiation rites, festivals, sacred spaces and objects and religious work of art; a religion which is slowly but constantly updated by each generation in the light of new religious experiences through the dialectical process of continuities and discontinuities. (p. 1)

This definition brings out the extensiveness and dynamism of ITR. The search of this work should not, therefore, be limited to the remnants and relics of an ancient and dying religious belief but should be extend into the religious expressions and interpretations of the overt and covert votaries of the religion even in the light of their new religious experiences through the dialectical process of continuities and discontinuities. By this we mean that the meaning of *Ịchụaja* shall be sought also in its expression by the descendants of the votaries of ITR even in their new religious experiences.

PART ONE

HISTORICAL AND CONCEPTUAL EXPOSITION
OF THE IGBO AND ỊCHỤAJA

Chapter One

Remote Antecedent Studies:
The Hebraic Connection

Apart from the well known theories of origins represented in myths of various kinds in the Igbo world, some scholars have recently advanced a historical perspective of the origin of the Igbo. Ogbukagu (2001), one of the major proponents of this perspective, elaborated also on the linguistic, cultural, religious, social, economic, and even racial similarities of the Jews and Igbo. He asserted in no uncertain terms that the Igbo are one of the lost tribes of Israel, most likely progenies of the Essenes. Ogbukagu (2001) aligned himself with the verdict of Abasika (1999) who opined that:

> [the Igbo] are the bonafide biological relations of the Essene Hebrew/Israelites of the Sinai Peninsular. Other Nigerian groups of the Essene descendants according to the same author also include the Ibibio groups, the Efiks and the Kalabari people in the Rivers State of Nigeria, among others. (p. 23)

It should be noted that the concrete historical data used to verify this perspective adopted by both scholars was informed by the so-called revelation through a self-acclaimed stigmatist—Innocent Okorie, from Orlu in Imo State. These data were given by Okorie in 1986 at one of his numerous mysterious episodes. The data insinuate that the great Assyrian persecution, which started in 722 BC, forced the race called *Shechenigbo* out of Israel. They sailed through the river Jordan and arrived in Cairo, Egypt, in 710 BC. There they were joined by other exiles *Efikdonaelis*. Both races made their way through northern Nigeria and the rugged Adamawa terrains to Nsukka, to settle wherever these groups find themselves in Nigeria today.

As at the time of this work, Innocent Okorie has died, but it could still be said that he was not a history scholar nor was he so lettered as to be competent to offer a detailed academic defense of this theory. We are left with belief or faith in divine revelation through Innocent Okorie for the credibility of this information. In as much as the present writer thinks that the credibility of this history leaves much to be desired, its specific details remains remarkable, especially when evaluated against the backdrop of the proponent's academic background.

Conversely, there are other perspectives which could be explored. Umeh (1999) went into greater details than Umeh (1997), insinuating that the progenitor of the Igbo—*Ife-nta*—made his way through *Ufo* or *Ekili* from the heavens to the present location of the Igbo. He rather traced affinity of the Igbo to the Ancient Egyptian kingdom and partly to India. This philosophical and historical perspective was augmented by Arazu (2005) with an entirely new idea of the Vedic origins of ITR.

4

Arazu (2005) had announced from the on-set that "we present here another plausible origin of Igbo Traditional Religion which does not contradict but accommodates other sources mentioned by experts" (p. 39). At this juncture, we dare make a case to prove the claims of Arazu. Ogbukagu (2001) had stated:

> During the process of conducting rituals or making sacrifices to the smaller gods the Igbo people often call on the Supreme Being to come down and intercede through these divinities to make things happen according to the expectations of one proffering the sacrifices. (p. 27)

This statement of Ogbukagu is in line with the revelation of the Bhagavad- Gita 9: 23-24:

> Those who are devotees of other gods and who worship them with faith actually worship only Me, O son of Kunti, but they do so in a wrong way. I am the only enjoyer of all sacrifices. Therefore, those who do not recognize My true transcendental nature fall down.

Arazu (2005) may well be extolled for his earlier claim to the plausibility of his own theory of the origin of ITR when he concluded: "The similarities between Vedic and Igbo Traditional Religions are outstanding, simply unbelievable" (p. 44). However, many features found in ITR upon which claims as to the Jewish ancestry of the Igbo are laid could also be found in other African religions. Specifically addressing this point, Awolalu and Dopamu (1979) wrote: "[It] is generally believed by the Yoruba that sacrifices to the divinities are really directed to Olodumare. They believe that it is Olodumare that must finally and ultimately accept such sacrifices" (pp. 122-123).

Nevertheless, if we fault the historical argument of Ogbukagu on the ground of the verifiability of the historical data he gave, we may not be able to fault him on the ground of religious affinity or similarity of the Igbo with the Jew. There abound similarities in the Vedic religions, Judaism, and Egyptian Mystery Religions besides, with ITR. Taking the three theories—Umeh, Ogbukagu, and Arazu—together, we do not see a contradiction, but a complimentarity. For instance, the essential feature of Judaism is monotheism, but Judaism cannot lay exclusive claim to that idea. Ogunmodede (2001) indicated:

> It is stating the obvious that the earliest four thought systems were polytheistic. In the eighteenth dynasty, however, an intellectual revolution took place. Amenhotep IV attempted to change the prevailing polytheistic cosmology and introduced a monotheistic cosmology, namely, a system guided and explained by a Supreme God. (p. 18)

Amenhotep IV, who was famed as Pharoah Ikhanaton and reigned in Egypt between 1379 and 1362 BC, did this reform at such a ripe moment as prescribed by the Bhagavad-Gita 4: 7-8:

> Whenever and wherever there is a decline in religious practice, O descendant of Bharata, and a predominant rise of irreligion—at that time I descend Myself. To deliver the pious and to annihilate the miscreants, as well as to reestablish the principles of religion, I myself appear millennium after millennium.

William (1987), describing the religious situation during the time of Ikhanaton, wrote, "The numerous other gods had overshadowed the Almighty in involving people by causing them to worship the gods through the endless number of competing cults, all served by a too self-serving priesthood" (p. 110). This statement of William affirmed the insinuation of Arazu (2003, pp. 6-31) that the degeneration of the priesthood to priestcraft always engendered reform in all religions, taking Hinduism, Buddhism, Judaism, Christianity, and ITR as case studies. Ikhanaton, like Gautama, Moses, and Jesus was an Avatar in Sanskrit language. Avatars are divine manifestations in the material world. It could be inferred that Moses was trained in the tradition of Ikhanaton's religious reform 600 years later and introduced this idea as the mainstay of Judaism. The monotheism of Moses took another conservative dimension that rendered the Supreme Personality of Godhead as jealous and non-accommodating of other gods. By this, the object of Judaic monotheism became a personality and not a nature. Christianity imposed Aristotelian thought on this idea of personality to the exclusion of numerous divine entities manifest in the world of men.

ITR seem to have retained the purest form of monotheism, combining the ancient Egyptian idea, the Judaic system of worship, and the Vedic polytheism. The study of *Ịchụaja* shows some similarities between ITR and Judaism. For example, Ogbukagu (1997—) stipulated the victim of the expiatory sacrifice—*Ịkpuarụ*— as *Nnefi* (cow) and *Evuni* (ram) while Lev. 4:13 recommends:

> If the whole community of Israel inadvertently and without even being aware of it does something that the Lord has forbidden and thus makes itself guilty, should it later on become known that the sin was

7

> committed. The community shall present a young
> bull as a sin offering. (p. 46)

In spite of the disparity in sex of the victims and the addition of the
—, the similarity is obvious. The liturgies of expiation are also the
same—, especially for driving away the victim, which ritually bears
the sin of the community, into the desert or *Agu* (Igbo).

Chapter Two

An Overview of
African Traditional Religion

Metuh (1987) and Arazu (2005) had decried the evolutionist idea that characterized the study of religion since Charles Darwin came up with the unilineal evolutionary theory that marked the 19th and 20th centuries. The theory of evolution was, from the beginning, set upon its way in understanding the Western world as the finest or highest ladder in the evolutionary stages. Western religion or Christianity, politics or democracy, economy or capitalism, society or positivism were considered the highest development of the human spirit and the standard upon which the rest of the world should be judged. The rest of the world necessarily came below the Western rung of the evolutionary ladder, with Africa at the very base or first stage of evolution. Within this frame work, Western monotheism was certainly superior to a purported African polytheism. African religions were relegated to the grounds of primitive, fetish, and magical practice, and the continent characterized by an abysmal darkness.

Apart from the argument of the lost continent of Lemuria and Atlantis, which Arazu (2005, p. 46) advocated, must be incorporated into human history or the diffusionist theory with which he (Arazu, 2005, p. 49) established the Vedic foundations of African Traditional Religion (ATR) as a means of restoring the African lost pride, a studied and formidable definition of ATR—advanced by Africans themselves—might serve the same purpose. Such scholars have attempted to define Traditional Religion. For Ekwunife (1990), as has been stated earlier,

> traditional religion means those living institutionalized religious beliefs and practices which are rooted in ... past ... religious culture; a religion that was transmitted to the present overt and covert votaries by successive ... forebears through oral traditions ... a religion which is slowly but constantly updated by each generation in the light of new religious experiences through the dialectical process of continuities and discontinuities. (p. 1)

This definition is rather extensive. The usage of "overt and covert votaries ... in the light of new religious experiences" means that votaries of Traditional Religion extend also into other religious institutions (new religious experiences) in as much as they, being within the dispensation of new religious experiences, still interpret reality within the specifications or world-view of Traditional Religion. This definition has a great implication for us in this work, which shall be seen later.

On the other hand, Metuh (1987) defines traditional religion as "institutionalized patterns of beliefs and worship practiced by various ... societies from time immemorial in response to the 'supernatural' as manifested in their environment and experience" (p. 17). Metuh does not seem to be perturbed by the evidence of the survival of Traditional Religion even in the wanton apostates of our time. Those same people who have apostatized from the Traditional Religion are still a significant part of it in as much as they still uphold the overriding supremacy of Traditional world-view and religious practices in the cover of their new religious affiliations. As an institutionalized pattern, "Traditional beliefs and practices," as such, if not extinct, must be upheld by votaries initiated into the same traditional religious dispensation and who actively practice it within its demarcated boundaries. The implication of Metuh's understanding is that the votary of Christianity, for instance, has no reason to uphold a traditional religious idea or be held under the sway of its interpretative influence. Even when such a person is found, he or she may not be categorized as a votary of Traditional Religion. We must note in passing that such individuals (votaries) and practices of Metuh are included in African religious past and could scarcely be seen in the present-day Africa. In other words, Traditional Religion, in the strict sense and given Metuh's idea, is a thing of the past, believed and practiced by the forebears of the present day apostates, who have abandoned the "outmoded" practice for a newer and more acceptable one.

We uphold the definition of Ekwunife because we consider the Igbo brand (ITR – Igbo Traditional Religion) of ATR as alive even in our present religious affiliations. However, Metuh (1987) cited Dr. Erivwo's contention in a paper presented at the 5th Annual Conference of the Nigerian Association for the study of Religion entitled *Alternative Captions for African Traditional Religion*:

> to deny the term African Traditional Religion to
> Islam and Christianity would imply denying either

that African adherents of Christianity and Islam who inherited their respective faiths from their parents are Africans, or that Islam or Christianity are African in their present expression. (p. 16)

Metuh repudiated this advocacy on the ground that the adjective "African" will undermine the claim of universality by both religions. We think that Ekwunife's definition transcends the arguments of Erivwo and Metuh. ATR does not need to encompass Christianity and Islam in Africa, nor is universality entirely an impossible character of ATR. We say, rather, that Traditional Religion is the various institutionalized beliefs rooted in a world-view, characterizing a people (defining them and giving meaning to their existence) and the beliefs they cannot by any means dispense with, which they carry as an indelible stigma into whatever religious affiliation, modulating itself in continuities and discontinuities. Consequently ITR, in part, does not contradict any religion; it rather offers such interpretation to any religion to make its practice possible for the people of the tradition. In part, also, it preserves its own cult systems, priesthood, mysticism, and philosophy that distinguish it from other religious ideas.

Chapter Three

African Traditional Sacrifice

Awolalu and Dopamu (1979) stated the idea of African Traditional sacrifice thus:

> Sacrifice is the act of offering an animal or person, or some object, to the divine Power or powers. It forms an essential part of every religious ceremony, and is fundamental to worship. Sacrifice is primarily a means of contact or communion between the divine and man. It serves as the best way through which man maintains an established relationship between himself and his object of worship. It is also valued as the most effective means employed by man to influence the divinity to be interested in human affairs. Right relationship with the divinity, as well as his favour, will be secured by giving him his dues. (p. 132)

Consequently the duo distinguished seven types of sacrifice:

1. Meal and Drink Offerings
2. Thanks-Offering or Gift-Offering
3. Votive Offering
4. Propitiation or Expiation
5. Substitutionary Sacrifice or Offering
6. Preventive Sacrifice
7. Foundation Sacrifice

It should be noted that the definition above stands as the common action performed in all seven instances listed. It is important to mention this because each of the activities listed above has a peculiar ritual process or liturgy. So, if in all there must be sacrifice, then the definition constitutes the precise action, which is referred to as *sacrifice*. The truth is that no list of types of African religious sacrifices may be exhaustive becaise the traditional African offers sacrifice in practically all circumstances. Also, the materials for sacrifice include a wide variety of things ranging from ordinary birds' feathers to human beings. Worthy of note is the fact that most of the time; it is the divinity that specifies what should be offered in sacrifice. Unlike the Jews, followers of Eastern religions, and Christians, the African Traditionalists have no elaborate temples and altars. This may be because the earth is a deity in its own right; therefore, the earth's mass is already a kind of altar accommodating other individual altars to other divinities. It is common to see sacrificial materials displayed on roadsides, crossroads, and riversides and on squares and spaces. Ekwunife (n.d., "Lecture Note") defined sacrfe thus:

> Sacrifice is that ritual means through which traditional Africans commune and communicate with God and other supra-sensible beings by means of transformed symbolic object or victims. The

transformed symbolic object of sacrifice could, either be totally destroyed or dedicated permanently to God or his agents or left to roam about in the wilderness and so on. Whatever form it takes, in every sacrifice, the African religious man donates himself to the deity and supra-sensible beings by means of a gift which is ritually transformed either by immolation or oblation. Sacrifice is an act of religion, a prayer. (p. 62)

Ekwunife brought out immolation succinctly as an essential quality of sacrifice. However there is no immolation without oblation. This immolation is going to serve as the focal point of our definition of *Ịchụaja*.

Chapter Four

Ịchụaja and Allied Concepts

Many scholars have embarked on the study of *Ịchụaja* in ITR, but they have also always had at the background of their studies various theories of sacrifice already offered by some western scholars like Smith (1950), Tylor (1958), Frazer (1976), Mauss (1954), and so forth. For this reason *Ịchụaja* has always been considered alongside allied concepts as one among many cult rituals. Arinze (1970) treated sacrifice in ITR under five headings:

1. Expiation
2. Sacrifice to ward off molestation from unknown evil spirits
3. Petition
4. Thanksgiving
5. Interior sacrifices

Whatever he meant by these, what is important to us is that he confined *Ịchụaja* to the second of the list above when he treated *Ịchụaja* under the sub-title: "Sacrifice to evil spirits" (Arinze, 1970, pp. 55-58), though in all fairness he meant two senses of the word—a strict usage and a loose one; however, it should be noted

16

that Arinze meant *Aja*. Whenever he used the full concept *Ịchụaja*, he meant the "strict sense":

> '*Aja*' merits the greatest attention. '*Ichu aja*' is the term used in the strictest sense to describe a joyless sacrifice to evil spirits... Father Zappa and Nwaokobia translate '*Ichu aja*' as '*sorte de sacrifice imprecatoire*'. Some people have even taken the word literally to show its full opprobrium. Since '*Ichu*' means to drive out by force; '*Ichuda*' to drive down by force; '*Ichunye*' to drive in by force; '*Ichu aja*'; would mean literally 'to drive sacrifice, something done to drive away the unwanted evil spirits. (p. 61)

Meanwhile 'to drive sacrifice' makes absolutely no sense. Part of our curiosity stems from the question of why it did not occur to Arinze that the whole idea of *Ịchụ* and *Aja* had been misconstrued. We are in disagreement with Arinze's insinuation because we think that it undermines the whole idea of ITR. Arinze then touched on allied concepts, like *Ịrọmmụọ*, *Ịgọmmụọ*, *Ịkpụarọ*, and so forth, but the ritual activity involving oblation, immolation, and communion (in some instances), he called *Aja*.

Metuh (1985) acknowledged former historians of religions and anthropologists in the names of W. B. Kristensen, Van Der Leeuw, Van der Vries, Van Baal, and Evans Pitchard; he also acknowledged G. T. Basden and F. Arinze, and his faithfulness to this tradition led him to conclude:

> The generic term for sacrifice in Igbo is 'aja.' ... The term itself seems to refer to the consecrated offering to the spirits. However, used with the verb 'Ichu'; (drive away), it refers to the exorcist sacrifice to drive

away evil spirits... . Ichuaja (driving away offering) refers to the exorcist sacrificial rites designed to drive away (Ichu) the evil spirits. (p. 60)

However, he categorized his study on sacrifices under four headings:

1. Sacrifices of Consecration – *Ịgọ Mmụọ*
2. Propitiatory Sacrifices – *Ịlọ Mmụọ* or *Imerịa Mmụ*
3. Purificatory Sacrifices – *Ịkpụ Alụ*
4. Exorcist Sacrifices – *Ịchụ Aja*

Elaborating on *Ịchụ Aja*, Metuh (1985) wrote, "A community which is plagued by similar misfortunes may offer a scapegoat sacrifice called '*Igbu aja*' (literally killing evil). The purpose of this sacrifice is similar to the '*ịchụ aja*', but the ceremonies are much more elaborate" (p. 65). Metuh insisted that *Aja* means 'evil' while *Ịchụ* means 'to drive away.' We ask why *Aja* in the case of *Ịchụ Aja* means 'evil' and in the case of *Aja* mean 'sacrifice' and consider this inconsistency a great source of concern.

Ifesieh (1989, pp. 240-241) more or less took it for granted that *Aja* is sacrifice. In his study of sacrificial theories, he enumerated some Igbo sacrifices that have no aspect of communion:

Aja Agwụ	Sacrifice against destructive spirit (he is at times ambivalent)
Aja Mkpe	Sacrifice for widowhood which nobody eats
Aja Mwụcha	Sacrifice for purification from defilement, especially before going to wars
Aja mmiri	Sacrifice thrown into water
Aja Ụgwa	Sacrifice against the dead people that cause deaths to the living
Aja Ọgbanje	Sacrifice against repeaters

Aja Ozu	Sacrifice for warding off death and dead people
Aja Nketọ	Sacrifice for marking a cut-off from danger of all kinds
Aja Omekọta	Sacrifice to redeem and reinstate a family lineage or a clan
or *Emekọta*	because of all the abominable deeds to their forefathers, mothers, and so on
Aja Akalaogeri	Sacrifice to ward off hopeless and senseless children
Aja Arụ	Sacrifice to cleanse abomination
Aja Ụchụ	Sacrifice to ward off bad fortune
Aja mmelido	Sacrifice directed against a person to harm him or her
or *Aja mmegbu*	
Aja Ntụkọ-Ntụkọ	Sacrifice performed for carrying away and dumping all evils that may be present in the family in a common place meant for it for everybody in the town or village
Aja Amaghị me Osu (Amosu)	Sacrifice against witchcraft
Aja Ịtụ Iyi	Sacrifice against thieves or defaulters of any kind
Aja Mọmị-wata	Sacrifice to ward off sea monster that is dangerous to life
Aja Nkwa Ọchụ	Sacrifice for expiating a murder case
Aja Ọkpụ Ụlọ	Sacrifice to guard against the bad spirits that cause a lineage to discontinue through childlessness

Aja Ụbịam	Sacrifice against wretched spirits that cause members of the family or lineage to be wretched, paupers, and so on

Not even this list is exhaustive of occasions for *Ịchụaja* in ITR. Notwithstanding, it is pertinent to note that Ifesieh insinuated the evidence of *Ịchụaja* in some other allied concepts in ITR ,which Arinze and Metuh tended to treat in isolation. What Ifesieh called *Aja Arụ* implied the ritual of *Ịchụaja* within the context of *Ịkpụaru* mentioned by Arinze and Metuh in isolation from *Ịchụaja*. *Aja Agwụ* is also the ritual of *Ịchụaja* in the context of *Ịrụagwu*; *Aja Itụ Iyi*, the ritual of *Ịchụaja* in the context of *Ịtụiyi* or *Ịtụegbo*. *Ịkpụaru, Ịrụagwụ*, or *Ịtụ Iyi* (or *Ịtụ Egbo*) are allied concepts with *Ịchụaja*, which in turn contains *Ịchụaja* as moments in their rituals. What really constitutes *Ịchụaja*? Not most certainly 'driving away evil.'

Being the earliest in this school of thought, Basden (1966) seemed to have ignited this idea when he wrote:

> We note that "Ichu-aja" is offered to malevolent spirits only; there is no form of direct sacrifice to the Supreme Being. Annually – in July – when food is scarcer than at any other time of the year, a feast is held in honour of "Chi", and this is known as "Aja Chi"; but' though the word for sacrifice is used, it is a loose way of using. (p. 59)

Perhaps Basden was led into this quagmire because he had earlier understood *Ịchụaja* and *Ịchụogbunuke* to be one and the same thing (Basden, 1966, p. 57). We rather think that *Ịchụogbunuke* is what the votaries achieve by performing *Ịchụaja*. We think that *Ogbunuke* and *Aja* are not the same thing and *Ịchụ* does not imply the same thing in both contexts. The same Basden (1966) gave us a clue when he wrote, "Priests are known by the following terms. *Onye-Nchu-aja* or *Onye-Igbu- Aja.* One who offers sacrifices. He may be "dibia" also, or a sacrificing priest only" (p. 55). Again, we think that *Aja* is the same in both contexts while *Ịchụ* and *Igbu* are synonyms. These ideas will be elaborated upon in later chapters.

Chapter Five

Contemporary View of *Ịchụaja*

Though Madu (2004) was concerned about the theoretical underpinning of sacrifice in ITR in particular and ATR in general, we review his idea here as a contemporary viewpoint on *Ịchụaja*. Madu opined:

> In sacrificing to this High God, which exists for the sake of man, man admits his transcendency as well as his malleability. He can be manipulated to dance to man's own music. And this brings out the religio-magico dimensions of sacrifice among the Igbos. (p. 132)

Madu (2004) understood man as the ontological center of the universe with God at the apex of the ontological hierarchy of being when he wrote: "The gods for instance exist for the sake of man primarily and not the other way round, and as such the centre of attraction in Igbo religiousity is man, his enhancement and protection" (p. 122).

Distinguishing between the religious and the magical, Madu insinuated that there are two dimensions to sacrifice: the first is the religious for which Chukwu, emanating as *Chi* and *Okike* is the sole beneficiary of sacrifice (directly or indirectly), with man acknowledging his supremacy; the second is the magical through which God is open to the manipulation of man. Madu (2004, p. 123) agreed with Metuh that *Aja* is the generic term for sacrifice, but was careful in asserting the far reaching implication of *Ichu* as 'drive away.' Commenting on the statement of Jordan in Arinze (1970, p. 34), Madu wrote:

> The statement … is an eloquent testimony of Igbo man's belief in his inferior position in the Igbo ontological hierarchy and of course man's ability to influence them to his own advantage. It spells out also the web of relationship of forces in Igbo ontological hierarchy, a net-work so inter-connected that makes the Igbo universe a complete fluid in which reality is viewed as unity. (p. 123)

The two implications to this statement are that man reserves the ability to manipulate the divine area and that the universe is all inclusive.

Therefore, we conclude in that same vein that man may not aim at expelling, driving away, or pursuing spirits, but at placating or manipulating them. The idea of manipulation employed by Madu (2004) is akin to conform or compel. However, Madu did not bother himself with the precise action that brings this manipulation to bear upon the spirits. Perhaps *Ichu* might include that precise action. Again, Madu gave credence to our claim when he dared bring Metuh's idea of *Ichu* within the context of sacrifice to the high god. In other words, unlike Metuh and his allies, Madu did not consider *Ịchụaja* as 'sacrifice' due to *akalogeli* alone. By using the word 'manipulate,' Madu did not appear to agree with the idea of 'drive away.' Nevertheless, we do not agree with Madu's manipulation, given *Afa* as means of divining the mind of the spirits. O. Okpalansofor (Personal Communication, April 23, 2006) asked, "*Dibịa na-agba afa, ọ hụrụ mmụọ?*" (Did the *Dibia* that divines see the spirit?). Ordinarily, this statement might portray the *dibịaafa* as a manipulator, at least, of his clients. However, it should be noted that Okpalansofor may not be implying the manipulation of the client how much more of the spirits. He is simply asserting the faith with which what the *dibia* said is accepted and believed by the client, in the conviction that he knows all.

PART TWO

SACRIFICIAL SYSTEMS

IN SOME WORLD RELIGIONS

Chapter Six

Sacrifice in Judaism

Sacrifice in Judaism is a vast subject that may not be exhausted within this framework. Sacrifice is at the center of the Jewish expression of faith in the one God. It is the most complicated but dynamic area in the study of Judaism and could be described as the most consistent element in Judaism. Though the temple was at the center of Jewish cult, it showed an enormous temporal significance after a series of vandalism, especially that done by Nebuchadnezzar in the 6th century BC and Antiochus Epiphanes (IV) in the 4th century BC, and the total destruction of the temple by Vespasian in 70 AD that brought overwhelming despair on the Jews. It was the Sabbath and sacrifice which sustained later Judaism. However, care must be taken not to depict sacrifice as the only thing Judaism is about.

The Jewish world view understood the world as dual-portioned water (Gen. 1:6-8). Yet the words *shachaq* ('Sacrifice directed against a person to harm him or her the clouds, the sky') and *shamayin* ('heavens') are always referred to as the abode of God and the spirits (cf. Job 36:32; Ps. 108:4; Prov. 8:28; Is. 14:14; Job 11:8; Ps. 148:13). The area above the sky and its waters is the abode of God and the spirits. The Jews understood the clouds and the sky to be a solid mass or block holding the waters above the sky in place (Job 37:18). The area beneath the sky with waters demarcated from the earth (Gen. 1:9-10) is the abode of man. Man is the king of this sphere. Everything was created by God. This God—Himself uncreated—made all things, but it was not clear how and when he made the spirits and angels who surely existed with him in the area of waters above the skies.

The Genesis account of creation took care of the physical universe while the existence of the spirits and the angels other than God were taken for granted. It must, however, be noted that these spirits, be they whatever, were in collaboration with God—the Creator—even at the creation of the world. In fact, on may not be wrong to say that in the account of creation, the God of Judaism presented Himself as a community or plurality. One wonders this monotheistic idea that has almost become the exclusive quality of Judaism. Commenting on Gen. 1:26, Arazu (1994) understood this plurality consciousness in the Jewish Creator-God when he wrote:

> The use of the plural form for divinity is further confirmed here. Hebrew language does not make use of the plural of respect found in other and modern tongues. This means that "let us" here is a reference to a plural subject (Elohim). (p. 72)

On the other hand, man is portrayed as the king of the universe, and it was God who gave man charge over the entire creation. Gen. 1:28 reads:

God blessed them, and said to them, "Be fruitful and
multiply, and fill the earth and subdue it; and have
dominion over the fish of the sea and over the bird of
the air and over every living thing that moves upon
the earth.

Nevertheless, the exercise of this dominion by man was based
on his ability to keep to its terms (Gen. 2:16-17). Unfortunately,
this dominion was ill-fated. Man, through the deceit of the devil,
breached his covenant with God (Gen. 3:1-7). The authors of the
Jewish account of creation, whether or not they presented the
progenitors of the human race as a single couple or a group of
persons, implied that this breach gave birth to a curse that should
affect all subsequent humans. Christian theology later elaborated on
this curse in the writings of St. Augustine of Hippo and St. Thomas
Aquinas.

According to biblical accounts, it was this fall of man and
his consequent incapacitation to interact directly with God that
necessitated sacrifice. The first of its kind was seen in Abel (Gen.4:3-
5). It is not our interest to explore the Semitic insinuations about the
sacrifice of Cain, for which he was rejected; we are simply dealing
with the biblical establishment of the accepted victim of sacrifice:
animal.

Israelites, like their Mesopotamian neighbours, admitted of the
natural task of feeding, placating, appeasing, and worshipping the
gods. Rattray (1985) indicated the seriousness of this idea: "Indeed
the very purpose of human existence, in Mesopotamian thought,
was to provide the gods with the necessities of life" (p. 1143).

Alongside this idea, McGrath and Imschoot (1963)
stated, the ancestors of the Israelites and indeed many

of the later Israelites themselves thought, as did the Babylonians, the Egyptians and the other peoples of the Ancient Near East (ANE) that the deity had need for food and drink, and therefore the best food and drink which they themselves used was proper to bring in sacrifice. (p. 2085)

Therefore, even before the systematization of sacrificial rites in Judaism, sacrifice was already an important part of the lives of Jewish progenitors and patriarchs.

A study of the notions and occasions of sacrifice in the Old Testament (OT) of the Holy Bible will reveal that there is no definition or singular mode of expression of sacrifice. MacGrath and Imschoot (1963, pp. 2082-3) gave us three possible rendering of the term sacrifice in Judaism.

1. *Minhah* which denotes 'gift' offered to men (Gen. 32; Jdgs 3:15, 17; 1Sam 10:27) or to god (Gen 4:3ff; Is. 1:13; Am 5:22,25). This word was to denote "cereal offering" precisely.

2. *Qorban* which denotes "dedicated". It could be anything ranging from farm produce to solid treasures, like gold, provided they are dedicated or set aside for God.

3. *Zebah* which means sacred "slaughtering".

The main offering the Israelite makes to God was the life of animals. It follows then that the commonest word for sacrifice should be *zebah* (Gen. 31:54; Ex 12: 27) just as the verb 'sacrifice' is translated '*zabah*' – 'to slaughter' while the noun *mizbeah* means 'the place of slaughter' or altar. Following the insinuations of the writers of Genesis as affirmed by Koch (1969, p. 77) that while Cain was presented as a farmer, Abel "designated a shepherd whose figure pre-suppose '*la passage de la vie nomade a la sedentrization en terre de Canaan. C'est le paysan qui commet le peche.*' (The passage from nomadic to sedentary life at Canaan. It is the farmer who commits sin). "No wonder the sacrifice of Abel the shepherd was pleasing to Yahweh while that of Cain the farmer was not acceptable." (Arazu, 1994, p. 84)

Consequently, it is immolation of a befitting victim that is the consistent factor in the idea of sacrifice in Judaism. A perusal of the modes, varieties, and motivations to this sacrifice will help us to appreciate *zebah*, 'slaughtering' or 'immolating,' as the consistent factor in the idea of sacrifice in Judaism. Rattray (1985) underscores this point thus:

> The most important part of any animal sacrifice was the disposal of the blood at the altar. Whether dashed against its sides, or smeared on its horns, this ritual act made the sacrifice valid; in fact, it distinguished sacrifice from mere slaughter. (p. 1143)

Having established the Semitic insinuation in the story of Cain and Abel, that animal sacrifice is the one pleasing to God, it follows that the modes of making this sacrifice must be firmly established in the life of this victim. There are basically two modes and three forms of sacrifice in Judaism.

Modes of Sacrifice

There are two modes of sacrifice:
1. *Olah* (Holocaust)
2. *Zebah Selamim* (Communion Sacrifice)

Modes of sacrifice will help answer the question of how the veritable victim of sacrifice in Judaism is offered to God. However, the how of other materials for sacrifice will be treated alongside their forms.

In that discussion, we shall answer the question of what, when, why, and how.

Olah: This manner of sacrifice is translated 'holocaust' in English. The word *holocaust* was adopted from the Vulgate which in turn had adopted it from the Septuagint. So, it could be said that 'holocaust' derives from the Greek translation of *Olah* (Hebrew). The word comes from the root meaning 'to go up.' According to De Vaux (1961), "a holocaust, then is a sacrifice which is 'taken up' on to the altar, or, more probably, whose smoke goes up to God when it is burnt" (p. 415).

The word *holocaust* in Greek means 'wholly burnt.' The sacrifice involves total burning of the victim, signifying that the gift was total and irrevocable. Hauret (1973, p. 513) opined that *Olah* was unknown to the Mesopotamian area but was later imported into Egypt. It is, however, evident that *Olah* featured in ancient times and the time of the Judges (Gen. 8:20; Jdg 13:19). *Olah* in the strictest sense is called "burnt offering." According to Rattray (1985),

> The burnt offering (Lev. 1) was commonest and most general sacrifice. Appropriate for atonement or thanksgiving, its purpose, basically, was to win God's favour. It was probably the oldest kind of sacrifice (mentioned in the Bible) and played a major role in public worship … and rites of cleansing. (p. 1143)

The offerer must be in a state of ritual purity and the animal must be male and unblemished. Birds (a turtle dove or a pigeon) must not be male. Everything must be burnt except for the hide of larger animals preserved for the priest (Lev. 7:8). *Olah* was an essential part of consecration. De Vaux (1961, p. 416) gave details of the ritual that included presentation of the victim; laying-on of hands on the victim by the offerer; slaughtering of the victim by the offerer (done a distance away from the altar); sprinkling, smearing, and pouring of blood by the priest; skinning and cutting up of the victim; and the burning itself, the victim having been cut in four parts. If the victim is a bird, there will be no laying-on of hands. Everything is done by the priest and on the altar.

Zebah Selamim: This manner of sacrifice is widespread among Semites. De Vaux (1961) translated this phrase as 'communion sacrifice,' "for want of a better rendering" (p. 417). However, there may be no better way to render it. Many scholars, like De Vaux, admit of this rendering. Other nuances of *selamim* (always in plural except once, *selem*, in Am. 5:22) or *zebah selamim* could also be rendered 'peace offering' or 'welcome offering,' as inspired by a Greek version of the offering. De Vaux contended that "the practice of Israel present it rather as a sacrifice of thanksgiving to God which brings about union with Him" (p. 417)

Rattray (1985) emphasized the social dimension of this form of sacrifice against the cultic dimension: "The peace offering (Lev 3) was brought when one wants to eat meat. It could be a bull or a cow, or a sheep or a goat (male or female)" (p. 1143). Hauret (1973) stressed more its cultic significance: "[It] ... consisted essentially of a sacred meal ... the faithful ate and drank 'before Yahweh'" (p. 513). In *zebah selamim*, the victim was slain and its blood sprinkled on the altar, the offerer, and the people with him. The priests received the right thigh of the victim; all the fat around the intestines, the kidneys, the liver, and the fat of a sheep's tail—and only the fat— were burnt upon the altar. They were Yahweh's (Lev 3:16-17) while other priests shared the breast. Then, the offerer shared the rest of the animal with his guests. De Vaux agreed with Rattray about the tripartite subdividing of *zebah selamim into types*.

Table 1

Types of Zebah Selamim Comparing De Vaux and Rattray

Subdivisions	De Vaux	Rattray	Reference
Todah	Praise sacrifice	Thank offering	Lev 7:12-15
Nedabah	Voluntary sacrifice	Free-will offering	Lev 7:16-17
Neder	Votive sacrifice	Votive offering	Lev 7:16-17

This subdivision, according to De Vaux (1961, p. 417), is based on the ritual procedures, admitting of lack of precise distinction among them. MacGrath and Imschoot (1963) indicated the significance of the ritual procedure common to all three varieties:

> According to the ideas of the ancients, the consumption of a part of the offering by the giver himself affected a union and fellowship between him and the deity, who by accepting the other part of the offering showed his willingness to enter into this fellowship. (p. 2083)

In *zebah selamim*, minor blemishes could be tolerated, and a female victim may be acceptable. The laying-on of hands, the cutting of the throat, and the sprinkling of blood are carried out as in the case of *olah*. All who participate in this offering must be in a state of ritual purity. The subtle differences in the three varieties of *zebah selamim* are as follows:

1. The victim of *Todah* must be consumed on the day of sacrifice (Lev 7:15) while that of *Nedabah* and *Neder* might be eaten into the second day, but on the third day, everything that remains must be burnt (Lev 7:16-17).

2. In *Todah*, sacrifice is to be accompanied by *minhah* (of unleavened cakes or bread), one of which is Yahweh's and reverts to the priest.

For the sake of convenience and in agreement with most scholars, we mention that *Todah, Nedabah* and *Neder* are types of *zebah selamim,* yet they shall be treated under principal forms of sacrifice under this subtitle, which will help us place the subdivisions in their right perspectives.

Forms of Sacrifice

Thank Offering: Psalm 107 stipulates four occasions in which a thank offering can be offered:

1. Successful passage through the desert
2. Release from prison
3. Recovery from serious illness
4. Surviving a storm at sea

Psalm 19 typifies a thanksgiving of a royalty. The choice of praise sacrifice of De Vaux is appropriate considering the modal structure of thanksgiving: thanksgiving to God is at its apex with praise to Him.

Votive Offering: This offering is given to repay a vow that has earlier been made to a deity, as in the case of Jephthah (Jdg. 11:39). In as much as Jephthah's vow is voluntary, the actual sacrifice is a repay (Ps 116:14). 2Sam 15:7-8 shows Absalom asking permission from his father, David, to do a votive offering.

Free-will Offering: This offering has no special occasion; as the name indicates, the offerer makes to the deity a sort of donation for food (Jdg 11:31).

Forms of Sacrifice

As have been stated earlier, there are three forms of sacrifice distinguished by time, purpose, and sacrificial material. Considering purpose, the subdivisions of *zebah selamim* would have been appropriate here, but for convenience and ritual similarities they had to be treated as subdivisions of modes of sacrifice.

Expiatory Sacrifices: Dumbrell (1992) was interested in stating the hierarchy of the need for sacrifice in his discourse of Levitical stipulations. In all, he made this verdict:

> The conclusion is that the first priority of the sacrificial system is the need for sin to be forgiven. Personal consecration (burnt offering) follows a symbol of commitment, and finally the celebration of reconciliation takes place through the peace offerings. (p. 42)

If that is so, expiatory sacrifice could be said to be the most important form of sacrifice for a votary in Judaism. There are two variations of expiatory sacrifices distinguished by their ritual process:

1. *hatta'th* (Sin offering/sacrifice)
2. *'asham* (Reparation/guilt offering)

De Vaux (1961:418) asserted that the code of the second Temple devoted almost half of its volume to expiatory sacrifices, and wherever it did, it treated them either consecutively or simultaneously. However, their significance is not easily determined in spite of this elaboration.

hatta'th – The word denotes both sin and the rite that does away with sin's effect (Lev. 4: 1-5,13; 6:17-23). The expiatory canons of Leviticus gave five reasons for which *hatta'th* could be offered:

1. Unwitting violation of a prohibition (Lev. 4:2)
2. Rites of cleansing (Lev. 12:6)
3. Forgetting the ritual cleansing of oneself (Lev. 5:2-3)
4. Failing to fulfill a vow (Lev. 5:4)
5. Failing to respond to a public adjuration (Lev. 5:1)

It is clear that *hatta'th* is not a sacrifice of atonement for sin as the name implies. Crimes and sin against other people required ways of atoning for them. The victim for this sacrifice was prescribed depending, on the rank of the person—a public figure or commoner, rich or poor.

Table 2
Categories of Possible Defaulters and Prescribed Victim for Sacrifice

Rank	Prescription
High priest (public figure)	A bull
The people	A bull
A prince	A he-goat
Private individual	A she-goat
The poor	Two turtle doves or pigeons or flour

Hatta'th has two distinguishing marks:

1. the use to which the blood is put
2. the way the victim's blood is disposed of

It should be noted that the blood is the centre of concentration. Because it is a symbol of life, it merges the life of God and the offerer in a mysterious way. The rituals for the sacrifice are not the same because the sin of the High Priest, the king, and the community defiles the holy of holies while the sin of an individual person defiles the outer altar.

Table 3

The Different Modes of Disposal of Blood in Relation to the Weight of the Offence

Weight of sin	Personality	Use of blood	Disposal of victim's flesh
Transgression of the sanctuary	High priest or community	Sprinkled 7 times in front of the sanctuary veil; smeared on the horns of the incense altar	Burned outside the camp (holocaust)
Defilement of the outer altar	Individual: ruler or commoner	Smeared on the horns of the altar	Received by the priest

Note. Lev. 5:7-13 gave provision for a less costly sacrifice, especially in the case of a private individual and when the individual at the same time is a poor person.

De Vaux (1961) contended that it is not the case that the victim is loaded with the sin of the individual, as some scholars interpret, because the victim was eaten by the priest "as a most holy thing" (Lev 6:22). It was, rather, he thought, "a victim pleasing to God, and he, in consideration of this offering, took away the sin" (p. 419). Num. 15:30-31 makes it clear that sins committed deliberately are not possible to be forgiven. In *hatta'th*, we have a case of mere inadvertence to ritual or legal demands.

'asham. This represents the reparatory or guilt offering. The word *asham* stands for both 'offence' and the means by which such offence is righted. Rattray (1999, p. 1144) indicated that it was offered like a peace offering but for the confession of the guilt of the offerer and the repayment of damages together with a twenty percent fine. De Vaux noted that *'asham* can only be offered for a private individual, in which case the blood of the victim is never taken to the holy place. Lev. 5:18 gives the option that *'asham* may

be quantified and paid off in monetary value. It includes the value of property damaged by the individual. In addition to the victim of sacrifice, monetary equivalent of such property is paid to the priests—if the property is God's—or to the individual to whom the property belongs.

Vegetable/cereal offering: This is also called *Minhah*, perhaps because it was a vegetable counterpart to the burnt offerings. In Lev. 2, three forms of this offering are specified:

1. Wheaten flour, unbaked, mixed with oil and accompanied by an offering of incense. A handful of flour and incense was burnt upon the altar, and the rest reverted to the priest.

2. The same mixture of flour as indicated above, but baked unleavened and seasoned with salt, part of which was burnt, and the rest reverted to the priest.

3. The offering of first fruits, parched corn, or baked bread, oil, incense, part of which was burnt upon the altar like *minhah*.

The shrewd bread: Twelve cakes of pure wheaten flour were laid out in two lines on a table that stood in front of the Holy of Holies and was renewed each Sabbath day (Lev. 24:5-9). This was the pledge of the covenant between the twelve tribes of Israel and Yahweh. The priest consumed the bread called *lehem happanim*— the Bread of Presence—or *lehem'areketh*—shrewd bread—without placing them on the altar on every Sabbath and replacing them.

Last, the offering of incense is always an accompaniment in the forms and modes of sacrifice and can be a form of offering in its own right (cf. 1Sam. 2:28; Is. 1:13).

Chapter Seven

Sacrifice in the Vedas

An exposition of the Vedic world view will give us an insight into the understanding of sacrifice in Vedic religions - Hinduism and its offshoots, especially Buddhism. The ideas of the religions are made known in the Vedas—a sacred literature with the *Upanishads* and *Bhagavad-Gita* as its major components. His Divine Grace A.C. Bhaktivedanta Swami Prabhupada (fondly known as Shrila Prabhupada) has interpreted the Vedic teachings, especially of the Bhagavad-Gita, in modern times. Being the founder of the famous Hare Krishna movement, he understood the Supreme Personality of Godhead to be Krishna and that man can only be liberated through Krishna consciousness. In his work *Bhagavad-Gita As It Is*, Prabhupada (1984) wrote:

> Becoming fully Krishna conscious one is freed from
> all dualities and thus free from the contaminations of
> the material modes. He can become liberated because
> he knows his constitutional position in relationship

with Krishna, and thus his mind cannot be drawn
from Krishna Consciousness. (4.23)

In the Vedic world view, there is one eternal and uncreated reality—
the soul. This soul permeates all things, man and beast alike. Nothing
is created, nothing annihilated. Prabhupada (1999) wrote: "We
consider all human beings, animals, and plants to be living entities,
spirit souls" (p. 49). He rejected the *Mayavadi* theory of oneness
of the spirit. The Mayavadi theory states that the soul cannot be
cut into regiments, so as an individual is completely absorbed into
the universal soul at liberation, its individuality is completely lost.
Prabhupada rather contended that the uncreated individual soul
continues in an eternal journey, manifesting in different bodies—
physical and spiritual. Prabhupada (1984) wrote:

> every living entity is an individual soul, each changing
> his body every moment, manifesting sometimes as
> a child, sometimes as a youth and sometimes as an
> old man. Yet the same spirit soul is there and does
> not undergo any change. This individual soul finally
> changes the body at death and transmigrates to
> another body in the next birth – either material or
> spiritual – there is no cause for lamentations. (2.13)

The uncreated universe is a soul, and man is layers of body permeated
by this soul, and so are all other entities. The soul is in fact closed-in
by this body, to which the Vedas allot about five layers: the physical
sheath, the vital sheath, the mind sheath, the intellectual sheath, and
the bliss sheath. These sheathes represent also the levels of man's
self-realization. This self-realization is all about the world of man
and religion. In line with this, Arazu (2003) affirmed:

> The mystery is that everything man has ever looked
> for or aspired to is within his very core. Not knowing
> this truth, he wastes his life looking for them outside.
> Knowing this truth is knowing that by which
> everything else is known. (p. 3)

God is understood precisely as this same soul—Krishna. God is
not an objectified reality but all-encompassing, absorbing all and
absorbed by all. Murphet (1967) wrote, expressing this idea in a
saying of Jainism: "That which is One in Many, Many in One, yet
neither One nor Many—I bow to that" (p. 126).

Being this soul, man seeks God precisely in that which lies
within. The more he seeks the truth within, the more he abandons or
forsakes that which is material. The essence of Vedic religion is the
renunciation of materiality and the embrace of the spiritual within.
Prabhupada (1984) indicated,

> They do not know that no kind of material body
> anywhere within the universe can give life without
> miseries ... But one who understands his real
> constitutional position as the eternal servitor of the
> Lord, and knows the position of the personality of
> Godhead engages himself in the transcendental
> loving service of the Lord. Consequently he qualified
> to enter into the vaikuntha planets, where is neither
> material, miserable life nor the influence of time and
> death. (2.51)

Finally, there is also the idea of the demigods—*Indra, Candra,*
and *Varuna*—who are appointed officers to manage material affairs.
To the Supreme Personality of Godhead, the demigods are but parts
like limbs in relation to the human body. While man ultimately

dissolves into the Supreme Personality of Godhead in his religious pursuits, the demigods are also worshipped in the same worship of the Supreme personality of Godhead. As Prabhupada (1984) said, "When Lord Krishna is worshipped, the demigods, who are different limbs of the Lord, are also automatically worshipped; therefore there is no separated need to worship the demigods" (3.14).

But in fact, it is the demigods who are worshipped and, consequently, the Supreme Personality of Godhead. It must be observed that with the idea of the Supreme Personality of Godhead in relationship with the demigods, the Vedic world view gets more complicated. But this complication resolves itself when the scholar understands that the ultimate search in Vedic religions is for knowledge. In practice, the religion seems to be rigorous and ritualistic, but their efficaciousness of these practices lie in the level of knowledge attained by the votary.

Sacrifice in the Vedas must be understood against the backdrop of man's eternal journey and immutability of the soul. The votary of the Vedic religions strives for liberation from materiality through a series of sacrifices that 'purifies' the uncreated and unchangeable soul. In Vedic understanding, that which is sacrificed is always and constantly material, directly or indirectly. The nature of sacrifice is the giving up or burning down of material for the purification and liberation of the Spirit. The sole purpose of this sacrifice is to attain ultimate knowledge. Prahupada (1984) noted:

> The purpose of all sacrifices is to arrive at the status of complete knowledge to gain release from material miseries, and, ultimately, to engage in loving transcendental service to the Supreme Lord (Krishna Consciousness). (4.33)

43

There could be distinguished in the Vedic religions three modes of sacrifices:

1.   Sacrifice in the mode of Goodness (Brahmanas)
2.   Sacrifice in the mode of Passion (Ksatriyas)
3.   Sacrifice in the mode of Ignorance (Sudras)

These modes are categorized in relation to knowledge as taught by Prabhupada (1984): "for without attainment of knowledge, sacrifices remain on the material platform and bestow no spiritual benefit" (4.33). The material used in sacrifice is not considered as a distinguishing characteristic of one mode from another but the stance of the votary between ignorance and knowledge, that is, the devotee's level in his spiritual journey. The classification above is, in fact, the classification of men in their striving towards ultimate knowledge. The Brahman is born into the caste or level. Though Swami Prabhupada disapproved of this idea, the truth holds sway in traditional India-Hindu culture.

In the Hindu religion, the Brahmans are the priests and exemplars of the religion. There is also the class of those in the mixed mode of passion and ignorance (Vasiyas) and the lowest level of Canadalas. Like the class of the Brahman, the class of the Canadalas is also hereditary. One is a Canadalas if one is born into a sinful family. In Buddhist religion, these modes are options open to the devotee, a choice that he makes in accordance with the quality of his faithfulness to spiritual exercises. In spite of heredity, much depends on man's efforts. It must be noted here that Buddhism resulted from Gautama's revolt against the excesses of Hindu priesthood. These modes or hierarchy of men accord with and give meaning to the sacrifice they make and distinguish one class from another more than the value of material things used in sacrifice. For instance, a Brahman can make a sacrifice that has a greater spiritual value with a less materially valued item, like an earthenware vessel of flowers, while the Sudra with a more valued material like a golden ware of costly flowers makes a sacrifice quite less in spiritual value. It all depends on one's spiritual attainment.

The demigods are charged to manage material affairs. So as Prabhupada (1984) taught, "the Vedas direct sacrifices to satisfy these demigods so that they may be pleased to supply air, light and water sufficiently to produce good grains" (3.14). To an external observer, no distinction may be made between the modes of sacrifices because every votary is involved in the same form and ritual. What is performed is the same, but the effects are different. He who sacrifices in the mode of goodness is unattached to material nature, and in fact, as Prabhupada (1984) recommends, "all his works are technically sacrifices because sacrifices aim at satisfying the Supreme Person, Vishnu, Krishna" (4.23). In the full knowledge or consciousness of the Supreme Person, one's being and activity becomes sacrifice. This is the highest form of sacrifice—that which is done in the mode of goodness. As Prabhupada indicated, "O Chastiser of the enemy, the sacrifice performed in knowledge is better than the sacrifice of material possessions. After all, O son of Prtha, all sacrifices of work culminate in transcendental knowledge" (4.33). This practice of offering material things to the demigods is common among the Hindus and is done quite frequently. Some votaries who have not transcended the modes of material nature also engage in this practice, being attached to mythical knowledge. Vedic religions preserve bastions of myths, especially concerning the various avatars. However, mythical knowledge is just the beginning in the votary's journey towards self-realization. Subsequently, if he "engages in unalloyed devotional service to the Lord (he) transcends the modes of material nature and is immediately elevated to the spiritual platform" (Prabhupada, 1984, 4.29). At the level of mythical knowledge, the votary does sacrifices in the mode of ignorance. The doctrinal exposition of the Roman Catholic idea of sacrifice may be categorized in this mode: ignorance. Nevertheless, the theological or mystical interpretations elevate it to the mode of passion and goodness.

Apart from the sacrifice of material nature, there is also sacrifice of devotional studies of the Vedas, a sacrifice that also purifies the devotee of the Vedas and the performance of the Yoga systems. Sacrifice—whether of the material (body), mind, or intelligence—is arranged to suit each devotee in his walk of life. Thus, Prabhupada (1984) instructed:

> Different types of sacrifice … are mentioned in the Vedas to suit the different types of worker … these are so arranged that one can work either with the body, with the mind, or with the intelligence. But all of them are recommended for ultimately bringing about liberation from the body. (4.32)

Sacrifice is, in fact, all about devotion to the lord—Krishna. It is the means through which the devotee is constantly purified for Sadhana or Nirvana. The Vedas even recommend the consumption of food sacrificed to the lord as a means of cleansing the devotee from sinful infirmities. In the words of Prabhupada (1984): "The devotees of the Lord are released from all kinds of sins because they eat food which is offered first for sacrifice. Others, who prepare food for personal sense enjoyment, verily eat only sin" (3.13). Gradually through sacrifices—that is, devotion—one arrives at nirvana because "sacrifices help one to become cleansed from sinful reactions of material existence" (4.30).

Sometimes it is amazing that the Vedas is given to a deep material interpretation in spite of its claim to a strict spiritual inclination. Material existence is due to the multiple reactions to human or sinful life. Ignorance is the cause of sinful life and of poverty - material, and spiritual. The paths of religion given by the Vedas are to enable votaries to escape material suffering and pain and to gain economic comfort, a regulated sense of gratification, and the means to get out of the miserable condition entirely. Prabhupada (1984) declared, "The path of religion or different kinds of sacrifice ... automatically solves our economic problems" (4.31).

The liberating sacrifice is called *yajna*, the performance of which affords perfection for the votary. Yajna assures one of enough food and milk in addition to liberation and perfection. Evidently, sacrifice in the Vedas has immolation as its principal character. The difficulty is that, given the Vedic world view, it becomes increasingly difficult to identify the victim of sacrifice and its significance in the exercise. The votary is at unity with whatever he brings to sacrifice and is, therefore, part of the victim. Ultimately, it is the votary who is constantly being sacrificed in lieu of total liberation.

Chapter Eight

Sacrifice in Christianity

Christianity has been reputed to be the major world religion, having substantial representation in all populated continents of the globe. It has a total membership of over 1.7 billion people. Any phenomenon as complex and as vital as Christianity is easier to describe historically than to define logically, but such a description does yield some insights into its continuing elements and essential characteristics. One such element is the centrality of the person of Jesus Christ. That centrality is, in one way or another, a feature of all historical varieties of Christian beliefs.

To understand the centrality of Christ, one has to make an in-depth study of the Christian sacred writ: The Holy Bible. Taking its cue from Judaism, Christianity accepts the Mosaic Law, Jewish prophecies, and writings. Christianity interprets itself as the fulfillment of Jewish hopes and Christ as the ultimate consummation of this hope. Christianity, having borrowed Jewish mythical thought on creation, advanced the theory of original sin. God created a good world and made man a sharer in divine reality. Man lost faith in God and disobeyed a divine injunction described as "eating the forbidden fruit." Christianity interpreted the fall of man as a shattering of divine plan. In the words of Suarez (1990):

> The level, secure bridge that linked earth to heaven, by which one day, without having experienced death, with no separation of soul and body, men were to pass over to the glory of the eternal beatific vision, was destroyed beyond any hope of man's being able to repair it. (p. 23)

The theory of original sin also insinuated that "what Adam had lost was also lost for all humanity" (Suarez, 1990, p. 24). Adam was the first man in creation, Eve being the first woman. Their disobedience of God beyond, being a personal sin, affected in the same degree all humanity that would proceed from them. This is the summary of the doctrine of original sin, without which the centrality of Jesus Christ in Christianity cannot be founded. As the *Catechism of the Catholic Church* (CCC) puts it: "We must know Christ as the source of grace in order to know Adam as the source of sin" (CCC No. 388). Of the Holy Spirit, Christ said, "And when he comes he will convict the world in regard to sin and righteousness and condemnation. Sin, because they do not believe in me; righteousness because I am going to the Father and you will no longer see me; condemnation, because the ruler of this world has been condemned" (Jn. 16:8-11). Further still Suarez (1990) emphasized:

> Not only man, but the whole of creation, came under the sway of the powers of evil as a result of the disorder sin had caused. It is not easy to be precise about how and when this happened, but we know by experience that any harmony between man and

49

the natural world is hard to reach and sometimes impossible. (p. 25)

Beyond the interpretations of Judaism, Christianity elicited from the same source the idea that humanity and the whole creation were in dire need of salvation, having established the universal effect of original sin. This forms the basis of understanding the comparison made by the author of *The Letter to the Hebrews* about the sacrifice of the old law and the sacrifice of Christ, the priesthood of the old law and the priesthood of Christ.

Nevertheless, Christians disagree in their understanding and definition of what makes Christ distinctive and unique, but they would all affirm that his life and example should be followed and that His teachings about love and fellowship should be the basis of all human relations. Large parts of Jesus' teachings, it must be noted, have their counterparts in the sayings of the Rabbis of Judaism and in the wisdom of Socrates and Confucius. In Christian teaching, Jesus cannot be less than the Supreme preacher and exemplar of the moral life, but for most Christians that, by itself, does not do justice to the significance of his life and work.

Jesus Christ was crucified on the cross outside the walls of the city of Jerusalem. The cross has become the symbol of Christianity but, most importantly, a sign of Christ's demonstration of His love for humanity for which, in spite of His pre-existent glory, He took on Himself human form and underwent the excruciating death signified by the cross. Christianity understood the death of Christ on the cross as the supreme sacrifice for which humanity could be admitted into the divine terrain. However, Christians are not agreed on the nature of this sacrifice and the mode of its effectiveness. It becomes rather complex to examine sacrifice in Christianity. In order not to confuse issues, let us focus on a particular group in

Christianity while bearing other groups in mind. We shall primarily discuss sacrifice in Catholicism while mentioning here and there protestant and Pentecostal versions in the understanding of the sacrifice of Christ. Even with this focus, sacrifice in Catholicism is still complex, considering the various rites making up the Catholic Church. Suffice it to say then that we shall lean much on the Western rite of Catholicism and its theological expression of the idea of sacrifice.

The theological understanding of the nature of the sacrifice of Christ takes its cue from *The Letter to the Hebrews* (cf. Heb. 4:14-5:6). The author of this letter, first of all, established the nature of the priesthood of Christ in order to state the quality and effectiveness of his sacrifice. Based on this understanding, the Catholic Church delineates two dimensions to the sacrifice of Christ:

Bloodless – referring to the last supper where Christ used the symbols of bread and wine to represent His body and blood (cf, Lk 22:14-20), not just to foretell His ultimate sacrifice but to institute a possibility for the re-enactment of that ultimate sacrifice.

Bloody – referring to His gruesome murder upon the cross, the actual separation of the blood from the body until water issued forth, giving up of life in ultimate obedience to the Father and, therefore, the consumatory sacrifice that guaranteed human salvation.

Pentecostal theology understands the Last Supper as a mere foreshadowing of Christ's suffering. Therefore, in itself, it is of no salvific value. On the other hand, Protestants understand that the Last Supper has the significance of merely calling to mind the sacrifice that Christ made and the suffering he underwent. Therefore, without the actual event of His death, the Last Supper lacks any salvific value. Nevertheless, having been energized by the eventual suffering and death of Christ, the Last Supper is but a memorable event not possible to be re-enacted. The Catholics interpret the Last Supper as equal in value with the actual death of Christ upon the cross at Calvary in salvation economy. In fact, it is one and the same sacrifice done in different manners. Catholics do not separate the two events in their relation to salvation. They do on grounds of chronology and the institution of the Holy Eucharist, the ever-living source of the re-enactment of this event—Christ's sacrifice—on earth.

For Christianity, therefore, there is one sacrifice and one victim and one priest. One sacrifice that sufficed for all things and all times; this sacrifice cannot be repeated (cf. Heb. 10:12); one victim who is Christ Himself, the one and only worthy lamb for sacrifice (Rev. 5:12); one priest who is Christ, above the old dispensation, He entered the Holy of Holies once and for all (Heb. 7:20-21). *The Letter to the Hebrews* is filled with deeper insights into the priesthood of Christ.

While this idea of one priest, one sacrifice, and one victim is acceptable by all groups in Christianity, the Catholics give a rather complex interpretation with their Liturgy of the Holy Eucharist. Catholics celebrate what is called the Holy Mass or Eucharistic Celebration, which they understand as a sacrifice equal in value and mystically the same with the last Supper and the Calvary event.

> When the Church celebrates the Eucharist, she commemorates Christ's Passover, and it is made present: the sacrifice Christ offered once for all on the cross remains ever present. As often as the sacrifice of the cross by which "Christ our Pasch has been sacrificed" is celebrated on the altar, the work of our redemption is carried out. (CCC, No. 1364)

The idea is that the priest who celebrates the Eucharist does so in the person of Christ and simply re-enacts Christ's selfsame sacrifice.

Catholics acknowledge the various sacrifices in Judaism in as much as they are imperfect types of Christ's sacrifice and stand abrogated by the same sacrifice of Christ. Christ's words at the Last Supper and the deep sacrificial implications of the bread and wine that have been essential and familiar sacrificial elements in Judaism cause Catholics to build the basis of the Eucharistic celebration and its significance upon the Last Supper.

Another side of the idea of sacrifice is that Catholics themselves, even in this celebration, are availed of the opportunity to sacrifice themselves with Christ. The people of God in the Catholic Church share in the priesthood of Christ, but in a special way, the priests have extraordinary share in his ministry. The words of invitation to the definitive moment of sacrifice in the Eucharistic celebration say: "Pray my dear brothers and sisters that my sacrifice and yours may be acceptable to God the Father Almighty." While the priest invites the people in the person of Christ, Christ is explicitly sacrificed, and the people, in turn, make of themselves a spiritual sacrifice in union with Christ. Explicitly, it is Christ who is offered and who offers Himself on behalf of humanity and all creation to the Father. Implicitly, it is the whole creation that is offered through Christ to the Father.

Christians do not offer Christ as a distinctive victim excluded from humanity (cf. Heb. 4:15). He is rather the archetype of their victimhood. By including oneself in the sacrifice of Christ, one is offered in such a manner that the former disobedience he inherited in Adam is atoned for in the obedience of Christ. Sacrifice is the unflinching obedience one offers to God through Christ, who is the ransom for the sin of humanity. All other practices of fasting, abstinence, almsgiving, and self-denial are physical forms of spiritual conformity with the sacrifice of Christ. The Eucharistic celebration is the summary of the Christian life and practice. To a non-initiate or ignorant initiate, the Eucharistic celebration might seem an empty theatre, neither entertaining nor participatory. However, the Fathers of The Vatican II council wrote that "the liturgy is the summit toward which the activity of the Church is directed; it is also the fount from which her power flows" (*Sacrosanctum Concilium,* No. 10)

In summary, Christianity accepts only one sacrifice: The death of Jesus Christ on the cross of Calvary. It is one, unrepeatable, ultimate, consumatory, and final. Considering this sacrifice on a par with the Last Supper and in obedience to the command of Christ, the Catholic Church extends the same significance and power to its Eucharistic celebration. The Eucharist becomes, for Catholics, the participation of the Church—His members—and the whole creation in the one sacrifice of Christ—the Head—through which he saved the world. All other aspects of Christian life and practice derive their meaning and power from this relationship.

This exercise of examining the idea of sacrifice in these three religions would not be complete if implications are not drawn from it. Sacrifice is commonly a moment of interaction between the human and the divine. In Judaism, this moment is temporal in a dynamic process; in the Vedic religions, this moment is eternal in a dynamic purification of a static soul; in Christianity, this moment is a definitive moment of breaking in of eternity into human temporal existence regarding which the dynamic soul has a choice. Most importantly, for all three and, indeed, all religions, this moment is characterized by a diminution of the material, physical, and temporal for a more spiritual gain.

PART THREE

THE NATURE OF *ỊCHỤAJA*
IN IGBO TRADITIONAL RELIGION

Chapter Nine

The Problem of Nomenclature

It would appear superfluous to discuss the problem of nomenclature if this work were a mere exposition of *Ịchụaja* as an element in ITR. On the other hand, if the work seeks within ITR a type of contemporary idea of sacrifice, then it may not be an endeavour in futility to discuss nomenclature. Motivated both by the works of earlier writers and the need to situate the new religious experiences of the Igbo within the elements existing in the Igbo world and Igbo world view in general, the problem of nomenclature is informative.

The issue here is that the Igbo have been stormed by Christianity, and the evangelizers employed available categories to interpret their Christian package and vice versa. Just like Arazu (2005) has recently argued that there is no generic name for God in the Igbo world, Arinze (1970) had concluded that a generic nomenclature for sacrifice cannot be found in the Igbo world. Nevertheless, this assertion of Arinze may be true up until the Igbo world was overwhelmingly influenced by western categories of thought. It is the Christian idea of sacrifice that Arinze found difficult to locate within the categories of ITR. Otherwise, if the Igbo must participate actively in the new dispensation of his religious affiliation, this generic name must be founded upon a reasonable conceptual analysis as had been done in various instances. Nomenclature outside this Western influence is far from being problematic because every ritual or religious act, whatever it is called, carries with it its entire significance within that same religious context.

Further still, the contemporary idea of sacrifice (at least in the Igbo world) has been deeply influenced by the Christian tradition. Christianity explicitly subsumed all possible nuances of ritual actions under the one sacrifice of Christ. In general, the various ritual acts found in different religions connote gift to the deity, expiation of the guilt of votaries, and life transmitted to the deity, which is subsequently conferred upon votaries. Christianity teaches that the sacrifice of Christ encompasses all these nuances. Therefore, either they are no longer necessary for the restoration of human-divine harmony or the singular death of Christ suffices for all of them. Thus, once sacrifice is mentioned in the religion of Christianity, no more can be seen in it than the death of Christ or its type.

The ritual actions found in ITR that have suffered this submergence are:

1. *Ịchụaja/Igbuaja/Ịsụaja* – Appeasement/Placation
2. *Ihunru/Irunru/Ifenru* – Paying Loyalty/Homage
3. *Ịkpọmmụọ/Itụalụsọ/Ịkwaarụsị* – Invocation/Conjuration
4. *Igbaamaonwe* – Entreaty/Intercession
5. *Ịgọmmụọ/Ịrọmmụọ/Ịgọarụsọ* – Worship/Veneration/ Adoration
6. *Ịkpụarọ/Ịkwụarụ* – Expiation/Purification

It should be observed that none of the above elements could be adequately translated as 'sacrifice' given the contemporary understanding of the word defined by the Christian tradition.

Basden (1966) seemed to have envisaged the problem of nomenclature in his treatment of sacrifice in ITR. He subtitled the chapter on sacrifice "Sacrifices," and in the primal statement of that chapter, he wrote, "Before proceeding to examine the sacrificial system …" (p. 54). In other words, unless the system is taken together, no single element within it can suffice for the more all-embracing western Christian appellation: 'Sacrifice'. To better appreciate this difficulty, an exercise in Igbo world view and some theoretical underpinning of the word are needed.

Arinze (1970) and Metuh (1985) we have said earlier understood *Ịchụaja* to imply 'driving away evil.' Their verdict was that in the strict sense, it is a ritual to ward off evil spirits. Arinze went further to designate its victim as despicable and offered without joy. He also admitted of a loose sense where *Ịchụaja* could be all-embracing of all other elements in the sacrificial system. In our investigation, however, there seems to be a consensus as to the nuances in the nature, occasion, and disposition of Ịchụaja itself. Incidentally, all those we interviewed in the course of this study put it thus: "*Aja na-awa awa.*" In other words, the victim of sacrifice or the particular object ITR—God, spirits (with or without shrines, good or evil), or ancestors—to whom the victim is to be offered, is not known until divined. *Aja* will certainly be established later as victim. Every sacrificial action is subject to *Afa*—'divination.' It is *Afa* that determines how, which, or what. To make the matter more complex, which spirit and what victim that fell to Okeke from *Afa* may not be the same with Okafor's even if both have identical cases to present to *Afa*. M. Ugwu (Personal Communication, March

2, 2006), a native of Obukpa in Nsukka division, contends that, in recent times, *Afa* may demand as much as a car, bundles of textile materials, cows, and so forth. It all depends on *Afa*. In line with this assertion, Basden (1966) wrote:

> To return for a moment to "Ichuaja", the offering
> consists of a selection of the following: food, strips
> of cloth, a gin bottle, a lizard, a chicken or kid, and
> other things up to a bull or, in the past, a human
> being, according to the instruction of the "dibia",
> and as the circumstances demand. (p. 58)

By *dibịa* Basden most certainly meant the diviner: *Dibịaafa*. He also challenged Arinze in his assertion that the victim of Ịchụaja is despicable and of no value. The present writer even insinuates that there is no strict or loose sense of *Aja*, it all depends on *Afa*, and it is *Afa* that determines everything.

In another instance, O. Okpalansofor (Personal Communication, April 23, 2006) of Akpo in Aguata local Government Area of Anambra State, asked: "Nnee ere I shi je-eje chụ aja na-evughu ụzọ jee n'afa? Ọọ afa je-ekwu ihe e ji je-achụ aja na onye e je-achụịrị aja." (How do you perform a sacrifice without divination? It is *Afa* (divination) which says what to be sacrificed and to which spirit.) *Ịchụaja* can be for different purposes—averting impending danger, healing, thanksgiving, noting anniversaries, preventing disease, ameliorating sudden deaths, and so forth. The list of this variety as found in Ifesieh (1989) has been given in Chapter Four. It does seem that the idea of *Ịchụaja* is consistent even in all other elements of the sacrificial system. Our interviewees all agreed to this idea when they said, "*Ịchụaja dị n'awaja n'awaja na-awa awa.*" (There are varieties of *Ịchụaja* and whichever depends on the stipulations of

Afa). Given the aforesaid, the understanding of *Įchŭaja* should not be mixed up with other elements of ITR that may include the idea of sacrifice. The nomenclatural designation of *Įchŭaja* must conform itself to its content and concept. In seeking this proper designation, care must be taken that one is not from the onset blinded by the idea of sacrifice popularized by Christianity.

Chapter Ten

Divisions of *Ịchụaja*

Beyond accepting this global idea of *Ịchụaja*, we think that the whole sacrificial system could be divided into two, depending on the mode. Leonard (1968, p. 441) distinguished between sacrifices and oblations from the point of view of the victim; Basden (1966, p. 54-75) distinguished between *Ịgọmmụọ* and *Ịlọmmụọ* while Arinze (1970) divided the concepts according to objects of ITR to whom sacrifice is made. According to Arinze:

> Following therefore the Ibo attitude, we prefer to make a division according to the person to whom the sacrifice is offered. This criterion determines the rite, the priest, and often also the victim. Ibo sacrifices at once fall into two clear-cut divisions (a) to God (rare), to the spirits with shrines, and to the ancestors ... (b) ... to evil spirits and to them only: these we shall henceforth call "joyless sacrifices" or "ichuaja", in the strict sense. (pp. 59-60)

Arinze's division is also curious because God, whom he acknowledged as the most superior in the objects of Igbo worship, gets either nothing or so little that could even be referred to as despicable in the act of sacrifice. On the contrary, we contend that even the priest of sacrifice is determined by *Afa* because the votary himself in some cases may be asked to do a sacrifice a priest might do in another identical case. Basden (1966) observed, "A man may be his own sacrificing priest on occasions. When, however, the 'dibia' so directs, the 'di-okpala' alone can act" (p. 58) Even here, Basden still meant *Dibiaafa*. So everything depends on *Afa*.

In this present work, we are going to make a modal distinction between *Ajanchupu* ('holocaust') and *Ajanchunye* ('communion'). The whole so-called sacrificial system or what we call ritual elements could be categorized in this manner because *Ichuaja* is virtually a common denominator to all ritual elements in ITR. In other words, we divide the ritual elements found in ITR into two, having in mind that *Ichuaja* is always and everywhere present in all of them. *Ichuaja* is a moment in the liturgy of all of them. The difference lies in the mode of *Ichuaja* in the instance of any. By *Ajanchupu* and *Ajanchunye*, we mean the division according to mode of *Ichuaja* that is required in the liturgy of any ritual element in ITR.

Ajanchupu

These are sacrifices which are meant to be wholesomely offered to the spirits, like in Judaism *Olah*. The victim of *Ajanchupu* may be consumed by the priest in some rare circumstance but never by the offerer. Therefore, in no instance may it be called a communion sacrifice. They are sacrifices offered to placate the spirits precisely when they trouble or torment a votary. It would not be in the best interest of clarity to mention particular elements in which this category of sacrifice is offered because, as we have already said, the priest, the victim, the rite, and the object of sacrifice depend on *Afa*. Arinze (1970) and Metuh (1985) will easily categorize what they called *Ịchọ aja* here, but Basden (1966) celebrated a rather complex presentation, showing that nothing is certain or strict and it is *Afa* that determines. The present writer affirms this observation of Basden. At one time, Basden seemed to be sure that *Ichuaja* is a sacrifice to the evil spirits, writing: "We note that Ichuaja is offered to malevolent spirits only ..." (p. 59). At another time, he presented *Ịchuaja* as an entreaty to ensure safety: "Another occasion for *Ichuaja* is prior to crossing water" (p. 59). To make it more complicated, he then presented *Ịchuaja* as part of the liturgy of all elements of the sacrificial system. Again, this last option seems to be more plausible to our investigation. The Igbo seem to perform *Ịchuaja* in all instances of ritual elements in ITR.

Furthermore, and as has been observed by Basden (1966),

> It is advisable to recall attention to the fact that the Ibo sacrifices for two main reasons. First because of the pinch of adversity in some form or another. In common with other folk, the sense of sin and evil at work in the world drives a man to seek help from an outside power whom he believes to be his guardian spirit. The insufficiency of man, and his consequent inability to walk uprightly, is recognized by the Ibo. This is really why sacrifices are offered. (p. 59)

It does seem that sacrifices of propitiation—appeasement (*Imedommuọ*), conjuration (*Ịtuarụsị*) and expiation (*Ịkpuarọ*)—attract deeper religious sentiments because such situations intensify, perpetrate, and sustain the interior fright of the Igbo—cosmic disharmony—and jeorpadize his religious effort everywhere and everytime to regain and restore cosmic harmony. This restoration is the ultimate aim of *Ịchụaja* and, therefore, religion. Basden (1966) judged rightly in the following statement:

> Sacrifices do not derive from any inherent desire to give, nor from any spontaneous love to render honour or worship. Sacrifices furnish the only way of escape from the evil designs and activities of malignant spirits. (p. 55)

Therefore, Basden was led to conclude that ITR itself is man's response to an internal fear which constantlt threatens because sacrifice is the heart of the religion. Arinze (1970) was in perfect agreement with the second part of this statement when he wrote, "Sacrifice is the soul of Ibo cult. If it is removed, Ibo traditional religion is almost emptied of its content" (p. 22). Whatever way the idea of sacrifice is driven marks the path of ITR. Although we acknowledge the statement of Basden, at the same time is not an absolute statement to be made about ITR. The Igbo also have the inherent drive to be 'master' of the world and strive to achieve this in religion.

In all, *Ajanchụpụ* includes all these act of sacrifice that is by their very nature propitiatory. At the same time, *Ịchụaja* is not as strict as Arinze (1970) has portrayed it. It is the climax action in the liturgy of *Imedommụọ*. For now we assert that *Imedommụọ* (appeasement), *Ịtuarụsị* (conjuration) and *Ịkpụarọ* (expiation) belong to the category of *Ajanchụpụ*, and it is *Afa* that determines its object, priest, victim, rite, and location. The common character of them all is that the victim is wholly offered up to the spirit—God, deities, ancestral spirits, or capricious and indignant spirits. Any of these could cause poblems for human beings.

That which Basden (1966 called *Igommụọ*, Arinze (1970) rather called *Ịchụaja* in the strict sense. The same element we now refer to as *Imedommụọ* (*Ịchụogbunuke*)—appeasement or placation because *Ịchụaja* has been identified as but a moment in all other ritual elements of ITR. Be that as it may, the liturgy of *Imedommụọ* seems to be comprised of *Ịchụaja* alone, except in some rare occasions. Perhaps ignorance of these rare occasions may be the reason behind the understanding of Arinze.

For instance, what the Amesi, Akpo, or Achina people call *Ajaezelu* or Amannachi people call *Anyanwụnaezelu* or the Awka people call *Anyanwụnaagbala* falls within the category of *Ajanchụpụ*. O. Okonkwo (Personal Communiction, April 5, 2006) of Okwurokwu in Amannachi, Orsu Local Government Area of Imo State, called this technically "*Ịdọ Anyanwụ na Ezeelu.*" *Afa* may recommend this brand of *Ajanchụpụ* for anybody. This sacrifice to *Obinigwe na Ezelu* is both an invocation and an entreaty. The offerer gets these items: a white cockerel, a coconut seed, a wild rope from the forest (*ụdọ agadi nwanyị*), an earthenware basin (*ọkụ*), the victim of *Ịchụaja* in accordance with what is recommended by *Afa*, a tuber of white yam (*ji ọcha*), one fresh egg, a raffia palm frond (*ọfọrọ ngwọ*) (the Amesi, Akpo, and Achina people use bamboo (*ọtọshị*) instead), and two feathers of a parrot (*abụba Ichoku*).

At Amannachi, according to Okonkwo, this is done only on Orie or Nkwọ days (NB: The Igbo reckons the week in four days – Afọ, Nkwọ, Eke and Orie). The coconut is broken and its juice poured into the earthenware basin. The offerer uses it to wash his face. The raffia palm frond (*ọfọrọ ngwọ*) is sharpened and slit in two at the narrower end. The yam is affixed at the same end in such a way that it holds the slit end tight together. The parrot feathers are planted on the yam on the opposite side of the palm frond forming a kind of the letter *V* pointing into the sky. The legs of the live white cockerel are placed between the slit on the palm frond and tied firmly with the wild rope (*ụdọ agadi nwanyị*). The other end of the palm frond is mounted on the ground at a suitable place in the offerer's compound. The remaining juice from the coconut is mixed with wine (palm) and placed beside the mounted palm frond with the wild rope tied on the cockerel's legs extended from the top to be suspended in the earthenware basin steeped in the mixture of coconut juice and wine. The egg is also placed in the mixture unbroken. The victim is now slaughtered, and the blood poured into the mixture. The priest goes home with the slaughtered victim after proclaiming the words of entreaty or invocation.

Okonkwo (Personal Communication, April 5, 2006) narrated an incidence in his family in which one of his sons often inflicted wounds on other children in the course of playing. The frequency of occurrence became so curious that he had to consult with *Afa* and was told that he needed to do *Anyanwụnaezelu* for the little boy. The boy's *Afa-ije-ụwa* (Astrological reading) revealed that he emanated from *Anyanwụ* (the sun), the idea being that he was orientated from and destined for physical might and valiance, which could be corrupted to villainy if the necessary *Ịtụjụanya* was not done. The *Anyanwụnaezelu* would serve the purpose of properly directing his destiny. After having procured the materials for the ritual, the *Nwadibịa* (sacrificng priest) was invited. Without a word to anybody, the *Nwadibịa* went straight to where the items were positioned and inspected them. He then looked straight at all gathered for the ritual (a few males from the family and the little boy). He then made a circular movement and dropped his *Akpadibịa* at what appeared to be the centre of the imaginary circle. He sat down on the same spot and asked the little boy to bring the *Oforongwo*. He prepared it accordingly and asked the boy to bring forward the earthenware basin and the coconut. When it was given to him, he held the coconut and said:

Mmiri Ezelu; Agbaghị agba ekughị eku

(The King of the sky's water; neither running nor fetched)

He elevated it as high as he could and took a hard object from his bag and broke it, allowing its content to pour into the earthenware basin. He put the fruit in his bag and asked the little boy to come forward. While he washed his face with the juice, the *Nwadibịa* said:

Anya saa, ya wụjụọ

Onye nyobe Mmụọ ọ fụ chi ya

Ị ga-egbu ma Ị ga-eji ọfọ

(When the eyes are cleared, they are more sober.

If you peep to see the spirits, you succeed in seeing your personal Chi.

You shall kill but not without cause)

The *Nwadibịa* did the other things with some hummings, songs (*mbem*), and incantations. He brought the white cockrel and touched the boy with it at various parts of the body. He tied the bird at its proper place on the *Oforongwo*. He then killed the victim [*ebili* (ram)] - *Ịchụaja* - pouring its blood into the earthenware basin while smearing the boy with some blood on his two eyelids and his chest. When the whole structure of *Anyanwụnaezelu* was set he said these words of entreaty:

Ezelu Abịaama;

Anwụ anya ya na-amụ dike

Ọfọ ka ide ji awa ala

Dike ga-egbu, ọfọ ka o ji ala

Mma dike daa samsam n'ụzọ; ya daa idumidum n'ụlọ

Onyeọma gburu ọchụ rie

Anya saa, obi daa, ọbara jụrụ

Ịhịaa! Ịhịaa! Ịhịaa!

(King of the skies, the Supreme Knowledge that reveals itself.

The *Anwu* (Primordial Being) whose eyes beget the great valiant.

The flood breaks through the soil with uprightness and justice.

The valiant kills and goes scot-free only when he is upright and just.

The knife of the valiant cuts finely in the territories of the enemy; but is blunt at home.

It is only the good man who can kill and make merry.

May your eyes be sober, your heart somber and your blood calm.)

At the end of the ritual, the priest announces, "*Ekele adịghị oo!*" ('There is no greeting'), and all participants disperse in silence. Nothing is left behind of all the materials procured for the exercise, used or unused. The priest takes everything.

Ajanchụnye

These are communion sacrifices. The major communion sacrifice in ITR takes place on the occasion of *Ịrọmmụọ/Ịlọmmụọ*. As has been described by Basden (1966) and Arinze (1970), *Ịrọmmụọ/Ịlọmmụọ* is communal in character. It could be referred to as the Igbo major festival. It should, however, be noted that *Ịrọọmmụọ/Ịlọmmụọ* is a generic name for major community festivals while the particular names or, modes of, and times for this celebration vary from community to community. It includes feasts in honour of deities or ancestors. O. Okpalansofor (Personal Comunication, April 23, 2006) observes that "*Ịrọmmụọ bụ ihe ọha zuru mee*" (*Ịrọmmụọ* is a community consensus affair). From our investigations, *Ịchụaja* is part of the liturgies of *Ịrọmmụọ* in all instances. Our interviewees found it difficult to dispense with the idea or term *Ịchụaja* in describing the aspect of *Ịrọmmụọ* when the victim is immolated and its blood poured on the deity or ancestral symbol. They always understood this part of the liturgy as *Ịchụaja*. In *Ịrọmmụọ*, in spite of the regularity of its occurrence, the consultation of *Afa* may not be dispensed with at any time it is going to happen again.

In Achina, Aguata Local Goverrnment Area of Anambra State, *Ezekoro* is the major community deity. It is *Ezeimo*—the priest of *Ezekoro* who announces the annual festival of the deity. Because the date is not regular as in the modern day calendar (though the season is), it belongs to *Ezeimo* to announce to the people the day chosen by the deity for the festival. On the day of *Iyiezekoro* (scheduling the Ezekoro festival), people gather at *Ogwugwu Eke*—the main shrine location of the deity—with great expectation. All the villages are represented especially by a number of masquerades for which they are known. The occasion is like a carnival, but the people are filled with euphoria because it is still the approval of the spirit that is being sought and one can never tell. When *Ezeimo* alights from the shrine, there is silence everywhere while the people listen intently to the mind of the deity. He may address the people in these words: "*Taa bụ eke. Echi bụ orie, nke na-eso ya bụ afọ. Eshi nkwọ e mee Ezekoro ... .*" (Today is *Eke*; Tomorrow is *Orie*; the next is *Afọ*. The feast of *Ezekoro* shall be on the next – *Nkwọ* ... .) People jeer and clap with joy having received the good news that the deity has approved of the feast. *Ezeimo* ends in words like "*Eke n'anọ ụbọ n'anọ ka e je-eme Ezekoro.*" (The feast of *Ezekoro* will be a 4-day affair). He raises his *Oji* (a staff ornamented with little bells and some talismans) and bounces it on the ground, shaking it to make a clattering sound. The people rejoice and disperse with a mini-carnival.

On *Nkwọ* day, people gather around the *Ezekoro* shrine. In the olden days, it is there that they cooked their food and made their feast in different groups. Before this day, *Ezekoro* would have made known to the people his choice of a victim for the feast. Before the arrival of the people on the feast day, some selected elders of integrity must have gone into the shrine of *Ezekoro* with *Ezeimo* to offer up the victim and make some entreaties. This offering is called *Ịchụaja Ezekoro*. Portions of the victim are given to the elders according to the social dignity of those whom they represent, while some are offered to *Ezekoro* and revert, obviously, to *Ezeimo*. It is these portions that are used for the cooking on the day of festival, and the people partake of the sacrificial victim. The rest is carnival with a lot of masquerading and dances that last for 4 days. On the 4th day, there is the *Grande Finale*, whose high point is the *Ịgba Mmọnwụ* (masquerade dance) display. This is an instance of *Ịrommụọ*, in which the priest of the deity stipulates the mind of the deity to the people.

Likewise *Ịrommụọ* in honour of the ancestors, done at regular intervals, depending on the community, takes the same form. The people either agree on the victim of sacrifice or consult *Afa* to do so. In Akpo, Aguata Local Government Area of Anambra State, the *Nguma* festival is an instance of *Ịrommụọ*. Two villages—Agbaelu and Uhuala—have their *Nguma* at *Owerre-be-ọkwaralakwe* (the courtyard of Ọkwaralakwe of the Ụmụọkwaraejimọfọ clan in Agbelu village). The *Nguma* is celebrated once in about 15 years. My paternal grandfather was born at the eve of the *Nguma* festival and was named *Udenguma* ('the heat of *Nguma* festival'). It was believed that the heat and clamour, honk and toot of the *Nguma* festival induced his mother's labour. On the day of the festival, people gather within the vicinity of the *Nguma* in groups, ready with their cooking utensils. Women pound foofoo and make whatever variety of soup they can. The men come with yams that will be offered to *Nguma*. The *diọkwara* (surviving first son in the order of succession) of Agbaelu village takes the earlier known victim to *Nguma*'s shrine accompanied by other elders, especially the *diọkwara* from Uhuala village. He slaughters it before *Nguma*, smearing its blood on the deity and on the sanctuary. While doing this, he prays especially for revived fertility for the women and health for the children. The animal is distributed according to *Ụmụnna* ('kindred') while the *diọkwara* of each village takes the *Ewe*—a choice portion for dignitaries. The animal is cooked there and then with the yams, and everybody take a part. A lot of food items and wine are thrown into the shrine of *Nguma*. People give generously and lavishly to *Nguma*, hoping to be blessed in return. In Akpo, people understand *Nguma* as a gluttonous deity, and such a sense is not unconnected with the practice stated above. In conversations, one may be asked: "*I na-eri, Ị bụ Nguma?*" (The way you eat, are you *Nguma*?) This sarcasm goes a long way to buttress the gluttony of *Nguma*. *Nguma* is also known as *Akwarị/Akwalị* in some Igbo communities.

The idea we desire to portray here is that the *Ịchụaja* in *Ịrọmmụọ* is *Ajanchụnye*—'communion sacrifice.' Apart from *Ịrọmmụọ*, there is another element in the sacrificial system that can be categorized here: *Ihunru/Irunru/Ifenru* (homage or loyalty). Arinze (1970) defined *nru* thus: "The word 'nru' means homage, but is almost always taken in a religious sense. It is homage, but which is materialized in an offering" (p. 61).

In *Ihunru*, as in other elements of the sacrificial system, it is the spirit or the deity that determines what could be given to it by the offerer. One of our interviewees—D. Ofuluozor (Personal Communication, May 15, 2006), from Nteje in Oyi Local Government Area of Anambra State, recounted that, when he went for the sawyer job, popularly called *ọrụigedu* (a corrupt form of '*e go do?*' that means 'will you do (may be this job)?') in midwestern Nigeria, he continually had the mishap of inflicting mortal wounds on people in the cause of even minor disagreements. Ofuluozor confessed that he did not do these things deliberately. He might want to hit someone mildly only to find out that the person had broken one arm or clavicle or rib. People suggested that something was wrong with him. He went to *Babaifa* (a kind of *dibịaafa* in Yoruba Traditional Religion) in Ijebu-Ode and was told to go and do *Ihunru* to his maternal great-grandfather, who also had the name Dike (Ofuluozor's first name) and had since died. It was believed that the older Dike *lọrọ ụwa* (the nearest English translation of the word is 'reincarnation,' yet all that may not be implied in the word) in the younger, knowledge the younger had been quite acquainted with.

To do the homage, *Babaifa* stipulated seven tubers of yam, a gallon of palm wine (*Nkwụ*), seven kola nuts, and a ram. At an opportune time, Ofuluozor took these items to the *diọkpara* in his mother's clan. Ofuluozor was invited for the *Ihunru*. The whole clan was gathered and the *diọkpara* introduced the occasion and Ofuluozor besides, who was not known by quite a number of the people gathered. He presented the items earlier brought by Ofuluozor. Meanwhile, the men of the older Dike's clan all came with kegs of wine. The ram was killed, and its blood poured on the spot believed to be the grave of the older Dike. This ritual of killing the ram, Ofuluozor referred to as *Ịchụaja*. Some encomiums were poured on the dead warrior, recalling his military exploits against the enemies of Nteje. Ofuluozor tried to recall some words:

Dike a na-akpọ ogwu n'anya

Nwamba azu eru anị

Ọkala Mmadụ; ọkala Mmụọ

Ị chekwaba anyị na be mmadụ; Ị zọọ anyị na be mmụọ

Nwa gi eruo gi nru oo!

Nwa Ofuluozor! Dike n'anya azị, Ị ga-adị!

Onye ọbuna ga-adịnụ oo!

(O Valiant, on whose eye the torn is nailed

The cat whose back never touches the ground

Half man; half spirit

You preserved us in the land of the living; you protected us from the land of the dead.

Your son now pays you homage.

Ofuluozor's son! The Valiant one of our time, you shall live!

May we all live!)

Meanwhile the older Dike was asked to sheath his sword that the young man may live in harmony with others. Some wine was poured also. The thigh of the fore limb of the ram was given to the *diọkpara* of the older Dike's clan; the back and pelvic area were given to the women of the same clan, and the neck and heart to the younger Dike while the rest were cooked with the yam and eaten there. Some food items were also thrown on the grave. Dike went home with his portion and one kola nut.

We conclude that elements in the sacrificial system as described above are not strictly *Ịchụaja*; they are not also strictly sacrifice. As in the Catholic Holy Mass, the whole of the liturgy is termed *sacrifice of the mass*, yet in the strictest sense, it is the liturgy of the Eucharist that bears the character of sacrifice. The liturgy of the word that precedes it, in the strictest sense, may not be referred to as sacrifice. So also in ITR, *Ihunru, Ịrommụọ, Ịrụagwụ, Ịtụegbo, Ịdọanyanwụnaezelu*, and so forth may not be referred to as *Ịchụaja*, but each has *Ịchụaja* as a moment in its liturgy, while in *Ịchụogbunuke* or *Imedommụọ, Ịchụaja* is the only moment in its liturgy. Perhaps this is the sense of "strict" that Arinze (1970) implied. If this is true, it becomes curious that Arinze (1970) and Metuh (1985) understood *Ịchụaja* as driving away evil and that *sacrifice* may not be comfortably translated generically as '*Ịchụaja*.'

Ịchụaja, from the foregoing, is the act of slaying a victim, ritually located within the liturgy of any of the objects of ITR. Slaying here should be taken in the broadest manner to contain the relinquishing of the life of the victim. To resign to this situation on the part of the victim in this instance is not a volitional act but a submission to a violent subjection. *Ịchụaja* is the highpoint and a recurring moment in all ritual activities of ITR. Thus, even when the victim is not slain physically, the dedication of its life to the object of worship is tantamount to slaying. *Ajanchụpụ* contains only two elements – oblation and immolation while *Ajanchụnye* contains three elements – oblation, immolation and communion. It is pertinent, therefore, to seek what makes *Ịchụaja* profoundly Igbo given the Igbo world-view.

Chapter Eleven

Situating *Ichuaja* in the Context of Judeo-Christian Views on Sacrifice

As has already been stated, it is Christianity that has narrowed the idea of sacrifice to the death of Christ. The older Judaism has a sacrificial system that admitted a variety of forms, as has already been discussed in Chapter Six of this work. Thus, Christianity made sacrifice (sacrificium) a generic concept in which all former varieties are contained. That is the sense employed by the author of *The Letter to the Hebrews* when he wrote, "And every priest stands day after day at his service, offering again and again the same sacrifices that can never take away sins. But when Christ had offered for all time a single sacrifice for sins" (Heb. 10:11-12). In other words, the one sacrifice of Christ suffices for all the elements of the complex sacrificial system of old and more so all the rites specified by the old ritual system. In this interpretation, derived from the Christian understanding of the centrality of Christ and his work, even in the very expression of the Church regarded as a response to the work of Christ, Christ Himself is still central. This one person, this one death is everything. Christianity also projected immolation as the principal character of sacrifice and interpreted sacrificial concepts in Judaism as such.

In the older Judaism, as in ITR, this problem of nomenclature is no different. We have seen that no singular element in the sacrificial system of Judaism sufficed for the word *sacrifice* in the enormity of its Christian rendition. Like the Igbo, the Jew has a complex sacrificial system. There are many similarities in the ritual procedures but differ widely in the object(s) and victims of sacrifice. While the Igbo have their religious objects as God, deities, spirits, and ancestors, the Jews have only Yahweh—Elohim—and while the Igbo sacrifice victims ranging from human beings to the most insignificant of material, the Jews do not sacrifice human beings at all, nor do they sacrifice certain species of animals. Prominent among the victims they use are oxen, herds, certain birds, food, and herbs. From the time of Solomon, the Jews worshiped in an elaborate temple with a complex altar and a formalized liturgy, but the Igbo worship in shrines and groves with simpler altars and without formalized liturgies. However, the sense of *Olah* and *Minhah* is evidently present in Igbo sacrificial system as in Judaism. For example, the vast sacrificial system of the Jews takes on the modes of holocaust (*Olah*) and communion (*Minhah*) while the Igbo holocaust may be slaughtered but never burnt. The whole victim is, however, given up to the spirit; even when the priest takes it home, the sense is retained, or when the priest claims it for the deity alive not to be tampered with by anyone, pending on when the deity decides to terminate its life, the sense of holocaust is still sustained. Many deities, even until today, have herds of cows, goats, sheep, and so forth. These animals are offered as holocaust: *Ajanchụpụ*. O. Okpalansofor (Personal Communication, April23, 2006), narrated this story to show the idea of holocaust: "When I got married so many years ago, my wife did not put to bed about two years after. I had to consult *Afa. Dibiaafa* told me that my wife's grandfather was asked by *Afa* some time ago to take a he-goat to *Ezekoro* in Achina, Aguata Local Government Area of Anambra State, when his wife is delivered of her baby. He went to *Ezekoro* and made his pledge pending on when his wife delivered. Later on, his wife conceived and was delivered of a baby boy but he did not fulfill his vows to *Ezekoro*. For this reason, his grandchild—my wife—will not be pregnant until that sacrifice is done. I had to take a he-goat to *Ezekoro* on behalf of my late great grand father-in-law. Once *Ezekoro*'s priest received the victim, it was dedicated to *Ezekoro*. The priest made some incantations with the kola I had brought and claimed the victim for *Ezekoro*. I partook of the kola and that was all." When asked what that action he performed is called, Okpalansofor snapped, *"Gini ka a na-akpọ ya? Achụrụnụ m aja Ezekoro."* (What it is called? I performed *Ezekoro*'s sacrifice.) The sacrifice of Okpalansofor could be categorized as *Ajanchụpụ*, which is properly an appeasement—*Imedommụọ*. It may be reasoned that *Ezekoro* is taking vengeance and needed to be appeased. Furthermore, the animal was offered in its totality (holocaust) to *Ezekoro*.

The varieties and variations there are in the sacrificial system of ITR are a strong factor for votaries. They allow the needs of votaries to be directly and properly addressed. They are as varied and variegated as are the needs of man, and so are the names by which they are known. Because the Igbo does sacrifice practically always and in all circumstances, it is impossible to have a glossary of the varieties of sacrifices there are because, as situations arise, sacrifices to addresse them are elicited. It should then be understood why it is that, in the new religious experience of the Igbo—Christianity—, this lack of variety is a contributive factor to the weak appreciation of the Christian message evident in the tendency of the Igbo to appeal to the seemingly abandoned sacrificial procedures in time of difficulty and even attempting to have its sense bear upon the Christian specifications. In a broader sense, the problem may be said to begin with the Christian idea of incarnation. The Christian idea of God-Man will be appreciable to the Igbo either in the model of a deity, ancestor, or legend. If it is true that this same God-Man became a victim of sacrifice, then the phenomenon is totally strange and incomprehensible to the Igbo mind. Then, if the Igbo were able to make this leap in logic, it remains for him to accept that this one victim and, in the Catholic version, this one ritual is enough to take care of all vagaries and vicissitudes of the Igbo life.

By way of analogy, the Igbo may understand the Christian sacrifice as a man with many names. That man will either be a bore or such a bundle of complexity that he may not be useful. Again the Igbo understand a multi-purpose medicine as lacking in potency; *ọgwọ nnụ ọrịa* is the derogatory name for such a drug. The Christian sacrifice smacks of *ọgwọ nnụ ọrịa* and will surely lack in potency in a fair Igbo estimation. Names in Igbo culture are a serious affair. They are not just tags: they are existential expressions of being. What a person or a thing is called constitutes the content of his, her, or its being. Unwittingly, the Igbo of today have come to understand *Aja* as sacrifice and are sure that is what it may be. However, there seems to be very little the Igbo found in Christianity that could replace or suffice for the perennial need of *Ịchụaja*. If we labour to justify the idea of *Ịchụaja* as Arinze (1970) and Metuh (1985) have done, perhaps the whole idea of it and reverence for it would mislead and wane. It is, therefore, important to give this name a befitting content and leave the battle of monotony that the

Igbo must surely suffer in their Christian affiliation and for which we shall suggest a solution in the course of this work.

Meanwhile, we contend that, unless sacrifice in Christianity simply implies the immolation of the victim of sacrifice, the word *Ịchụaja* does not suffice for sacrifice. Perhaps it is fitting at this point to talk about the contradiction and confusion the reader may be grappling with in our evaluation of the Christian idea of sacrifice. It would seem that, at one time, we say the sense is narrow, and at another, we say it is broad. It is rather the same thing we are saying in different ways. When we say *narrow*, we mean that the former vast sacrificial systems were compressed to be contained in the sacrifice of Christ; by *broad*, we mean that the sacrifice of Christ extends to all elements of the former sacrificial system. Either way, we are saying the same thing and are portraying the Christian perspective. So also *Ịchụaja* as a precise action in the various ritual elements of ITR is narrow, but as a recurring action in all the ritual elements of ITR, it is broad. The difficulty here, which has been mentioned earlier, is that, in as much as it could be impressed on the Igbo mind as acceptable that the sacrifice of Christ is sufficient for all the varied situations of human life, there remain to be found effective ways of having this same sacrifice satisfy the religious needs of the Igbo who are constrained to employ it. If *Ịchụaja* then aptly translates 'sacrifice,' the idea of Arinze (1970) and allies presents a terrible difficulty in the program of evangelization of the Igbo.

Chapter Twelve

The Theoretical Underpining of *Ịchụaja* In Igbo Traditional Religious Culture

Metuh (1985) thought that:

> [Aja] ... used with the verb 'ichu' (drive away) ... refers to the exorcist sacrifice to drive away evil spirits ... in fact in most cases it is the verb that determines the type of sacrifice as is evident in these four terms which refer to the different sacrifices offered by the Igbo: *Igommuo, Imeriammuo, Ichuaja* and *Ikpualu*. (p. 60)

With this complication, it becomes very difficult to borrow any idea from his subsequent assertions on the topic because the primal premise is considered erroneous. He included *Ịchụaja* as one of the forms of sacrifice, categorizing it by the verb *Ịchụ*, whereas the other three forms of sacrifice do not suffice for *Aja* in spite of the nuances of the verb that he contends is the principle for categorizing forms of sacrifice. Metuh's contention, according to the assertion above, would have been plausible if the forms of sacrifice were *Igọaja, Imeriaja, Ichụaja,* and *Ikpụaja,* but apart from *Ichụaja,* the rest as just coined are nonsensical to the Igbo. Metuh's case cannot be clarified even by him.

On the other hand, *Ichụ* could also mean 'to slay.' The difference between *Ichụ,* 'to drive away,' and *Ichụ,* 'to slay,' is simply tonal and syntactic. Nevertheless, tonality could be mutable through time. Arinze (1970) and Metuh (1985) may not have considered this possibility of mutation when they understood *Ichụ* simply as 'to drive away.' Apart from tonality, there is a further argument from the sytactic expression of these words. Table 4 displays the phonological-syntactic variations or concordance of the words in various Igbo cultural areas to help to clarify this matter.

Table 4
Phonological and Syntactic Variations of Ichụ as Associated with Ichụaja

Area	Town	'To drive away'	'To slay'	'To offer in sacrifice'
Northern Igbo	Obukpa	Ichụ	Ichụ/Igbu	Ichụaja/Igbuaja
North central Igbo	Akpo	Ichụ	Ich-hụ /Igbu	Ichụaja
South central Igbo	Akokwa	Ichụ	Ich-hụ/Is-hụ/ Igbu	Ichụaja/Is-hụaja
North western Igbo	Nnewi	Ichụ	Ichụ /Igbu	Ichụaja
North western Igbo	Eziowelle	Ichụ	Ichụ /Igbu	Ichụaja

As shown in Table 4, the Obukpa people in Nsukka area present a problem for the conclusion of Arinze (1970) and Metuh (1985). *Igbuaja* will literally mean 'slaying Aja.' Basden (1966) also gave this curious statement: "Priests are known by the following terms: Onye-nchu-aja or Onye-igbu-aja. One who offers sacrifices. He may be a 'dibia' also, or a sacrificing priest only" (p. 55). Second, for the Akpo people in Aguata Local Government Area, in pronouncing the word *Ichu* as in sacrifice, there is a salient *h* that escapes through the nasal air passage: *Ich-hu*. However, if it were *Ichu* as in 'to pursue' or 'drive away,' the diphthong *ch* would not have such complicated pronunciation. Also, the word *Ichu* as in 'slaying' has such complication as does *Ichu* as in 'sacrifice.' Third, the Akokwa people in Ideato North Local Government Area of Imo State render the word for slaying in two forms *Ichu* and *Isu*. Either way, in pronouncing those words, there is evidence of that complication of a silent *h*. Again, the other alternative *Isu* exists in the form of *Isuaja*—'sacrifice'—but never in the form of *Isuoso*— 'to drive away.'

Finally, in the Catholic penny Catechism of the Owerri ecclesiastical area of Imo State, the question *"Gini bu aja?"* (What is *Aja*?) is answered with *"Aja bu iji 'victim' huoro Chineke site n'aka Priest."* (*Aja* is the offering of a victim to God through the hands of the priest.) It is upon this foundation that we construct the fundamental idea of immolation in *Ichuaja*. *Ichuaja* simply put is 'the slaying of the victim.' The significance of this slaying is contained within the concept. Strictly speaking then, *Ichuaja* may conveniently translate as 'sacrifice' in Igbo only if *sacrifice* is narrowed to mean the slaying of the victim alone. But the slaying of the victim is the production of blood, which is the symbol of life. Ultimately, it is the life of the offerer that is spiritually conformed to the life of the object of religion in all ritual elements. This conformity of life is ritually demonstrated in the subduing of the victim and its consequent submission of its life in accordance to the will of the priest who overpowers it.

Nevertheless, the thought of Arinze (1970) that the victim of *Ịchụaja* is despicable is not totally unfounded however, if it were just a question of the infinitesimal nature of the victim, then it is wrong. On the other hand, which may be more acceptable, even if it is a human being who will be used as the victim, the human being is despicable. The sense here was given by Isaiah (cf. Is. 52:14-53:12). It is the nature of every possible victim to be contemptible, despicable, dejected, forsaken, forlorn, and defeated. This idea of being hopelessly terrified and treated inhumanly to the extent of extinguishing life smacks of the worthlessness of the life of the victim. Its life is no longer evaluated at the same price and quality as other lives. If Arinze meant by his assertion that the victim of *Ịchụaja* is totally worthless and despicable, then we are in perfect agreement with him. At the same time, if that is the case, a classification, then, that is based on the victim is bound to be problematic. To be worthless and despicable is a necessary quality of any victim of sacrifice and cannot be a mark of distinction. On the other hand, if worthless and deispicable is understood from a quantitative perspective, then even Chukwu—the highest being—may have a day old chick as a victim while *Haaba*—a mere deity—gets a cow. Is that not curious!

In the long run, it is the violence done to the victim, to gain access to its life, which makes the blood flow. That blood is a sign of the restoration of divine-human concord. In a broader sense, immolation is done in accordance with the nature of the victim. Immolation may not always produce blood in the physical sense of the word. Can wine or a kola nut, for instance, be slain? But they can be used for sacrifice in an immolation sense. Their being poured or thrown ritually onto the earth, to the deity, or onto a sacred space is a form of immolation because they bear in that act a denigration of their social and ritual dignity; they are worthless and despicable.

Immolation brings out the practical nature of sacrifice. It remains to be asked whether what is seen is all there is to the idea of sacrifice. To take care of this concern, the exteriority and interiority of the sacrificial action need to be explored. *Exteriority* has to do with the act as perceived through the senses while *interiority* has to do with the act as signified or symbolized.

PART FOUR

ỊCHỤAJA IN THE CONTEXT OF
IGBO WORLD VIEW

Chapter Thirteen

Igbo Pre-Historic Excursus

Like the Babylonians, the Indians, and indeed every culture of the world, the Igbo have myths of origins of the world and things in it. We deem it fit in this section to do some analysis of existing cosmogonies before eliciting from it the elements of the Igbo world view. Nevertheless, it is our wish to make a case for pre-historic excursus within the arena of what we had known as cosmogony and theogony. Over and above that, we also desire to attempt a conceptual analysis, placing these myths in a comparative stance with the more popular biblical creation story. To allude to these myths as pre-history will allow for projecting and laying out the Igbo religious experience as one strand of historical events coloured by periodical influences, but consistently bearing a unique character. Such historical continuity will give us the dynamics in history that shaped the Igbo religious experience. Igbo cosmogonies and theogonies have been studied in isolation by anthropologists, ethnologists, scholars of religion, and philosophers with far-reaching implications, but the biblical model of recording religious experiences affords the scholar easy access to the people, time, and events that constitute such experiences as if it were one strand of events.

The idea of "pre-historic" is taken from biblical scholars' description of stories in Gen. 1-11. The basic idea of scholars is that the story entries of the earliest portion of the Christian scripture followed the mythical pattern of the Ancient near East (ANE). According to Clifford and Murphy (1995),

> In Mesopotamian culture, evidently the model for most of the stories in Gen. 1-11, scribes explored beginnings through stories and cosmogonies not through abstract reasoning. Most of the extant Mesopotamian cosmogonies are belief, but there are several extended compositions that collect accounts of origins, the Gilgamesh Epic, Enuma Elish and Atrahasis Story. (p. 8)

For instance, the Atrahasis Story has it that a disputation among the gods brought about the creation of humans by a dissident spirit. The offending of the gods by humans brought about the great flood through successive plagues. The offence of the humans tagged *noise* was not specifically classified as moral but is implied. In the consequent destruction of the human race that followed, a divine favourite—Utnapishtim—was spared. Observe that the details of the story ape Gen. 2-9 (Clifford & Murphy, p. 8).

The beginning and high-point of the story of Israel is the miraculous liberation from Egyptian bondage (Ex. 12) and the events around the foot of Mount Sinai, especially the covenant (Ex. 19-20), by which Israel became a definite people constituted by God. The earliest written record about this people is the code of this covenant. The stories that precede Ex. 19 (the Covenant at Sinai) from Gen. 12 (The call of Abram) were background stories (though not entirely lacking in historical credibility) to establish this definitive emergence of the Abrahamic people of promise (Clifford & Murphy, 1995, p. 18-19). On the other hand, Gen. 1 (Creation narrative) to Gen. 11 (The Tower of Babel and the Dispersion of "the sons of men" on earth) is properly called pre-history because it filled in the background story, and without it, the entire story would have lacked in historical continuity. However, the continuity achieved is not enough to prove the scientific verifiability of the details of the story. Nevertheless, the truth remains that this background story is an eclectic edition of already existing cosmogonies and myths in the ANE of the time (Charpentier, 1993, p. 18). Israel simply appropriated them and, thus, became custodian of quite a number of them, not without readapting them to its very situation. Yet in spite of the work of Israelite editors and redactors, the various traditions that make up the hagiography can still easily be seen.

It is this understanding of pre-history that we seek to employ in analyzing Igbo cosmogonies and myths as they pertain to the origins. From the onset, it needs to be made clear that "the Igbo lack a common tradition of origin. Each village group having a self-awareness of unity traces its origin to an ancestor and/or to a ritual event constituting it into an entity" (Uzukwu, 1988, p. 92). This assertion is no less a truth for the people of ANE and even Israel itself. Like the various strands of thought put together in the biblical account of creation of the human race and the establishment of the Israelite nation, the Igbo myths of the origins comprise of various versions. For now, writers generally allude to four popular versions:

1. Nri Cosmogony
2. Ibagwa Theogony
3. Delta Group Creation Account
4. Mbaise Cosmogony

A thorough reading of these versions shows that each has a particular interest in its attempt to establish its own people. Though interests may clash from place to place, one may exercise dominance over another in their particularities. However, it is possible, like biblical editors, to bring these stories into a single focus. Until that is done, these stories are still within the tradition of cosmogonies. It is pertinent to address this so-called pre-history in this work in order to establish the place of God, the gods and deities, spirits, and men in the Igbo universe before determining Igbo cultic systems. Doing so will shed a clear light on what the Igbo basically thinks of themselves in relation to the world around them.

Again, like the priestly tradition of the Judeo-Christian Biblical composition, the Nri cosmogony presents the Igbo as a priestly people who not only are constituted to play a cultic role in creation but also are especially called to have a special communion with God. However, it must be admitted that the myth in question, at face value, may not have broadly presented itself in such universal categories except that the Nri is interpreted as the prototype of the Igbo race while Eri is the archetype and progenitor: a type of Adam.

Perhaps the Igbo have no thought of absolute nothing. Like other ancient cultures and traditions, Igbo myths, cosmogonies, and theogonies are attempts at interpreting that world that presented itself to the agitated Igbo mind. Generally, myths, cosmogonies, and theogonies give credence to religious truths. Metuh (1981) asserted, "[Myth] ... enhances the values as authentic vehicles of religious beliefs, since such beliefs would enjoy an appreciable degree of authenticity" (p. 28). Not even the Ibagwa theogonic myth (Metuh, 1981, p. 33), which tried to make God create the earth, the sky, and celestial bodies, was able to give details, but overwhelmed by the awe of origins, presumed that God made them, without details of how, like the second account of creation in the Christian Bible. So, the fact of the material world can only be resolved in God who made things for different purposes.

The Nri creation myth showed the difficulty of the Igbo in reducing the world of material facticity to nothing (Metuh, 1981, p. 29), so it also presumed the sky and the earth. The three ancestors that generated the Igbo race—Eri, Dioka, and Oka—were sent to earth from the sky by God. Eri, who was the eldest and of a superior personality of them all, came down to earth, which was in the form of a morass (*ala dị deke deke*). Eri and Nri, his son, like the Israelites were fed with a heavenly food, *Azụigwe* (manna in the case of Israel). Also, Nri like Abraham, who had three visitors, had four visitors from Chukwu (Obinigwe): spiritual personages who became the animating spirits of the 4-day Igbo week (Afọ, Nkwọ, Eke, and Orie are names of days of the week as well as deities). In every Igbo village, there is a shrine in the market place where sacrifices are made to specific market deities bearing each as name a day of the week when the people of the village engage in serious commercial activities.

When there was still an uninterrupted communion between the human and the divine world (while Eri still lived), there was no need for the separation of day and night, giving a natural case for temporality. Even the Igbo had a sense of timelessness of God and the realm of the spirits. Another point is that Nri's heavenly visitors were dealers of *Azụ* (*Azụ* is fish. It reminds us of *Azụigwe*. The Nri myth might have been composed in a riverine area where *Azụ* is a common food. Thus, Azụigwe might be these people's version of the "bread of heaven"). The heavenly fish, *Azụigwe*, ceased to be available with the death of Eri, and Nri had to ask for an earthly alternative, which came in the forms of *Ji* (yam), *Ede* (cocoyam), *Akwụ* (palm), and *Ụkwa* (breadfruit), which are the Igbo staple food items that have religious significance. The Nri myth does not tell us the cause of the cessation of the supply of *Azụigwe*, but further search into related stories most certainly reveal that the rupture of this harmonious human-divine concourse was caused by a moral misconduct on the part of humans. Death, evil, and the suffering of humans are always given such origins in mythical explanations.

The Nri myth does not conceive a peopleless world, unlike the Judeo-Christian biblical narrative, but a world where Eri is the ideal man (Uzukwu, 1988, p. 95). One can easily observe immediately that what agitated the Nri mind were cosmological, geographical, economic, and sociological questions. However, they were within the given itinerant priestly role, which they already played among the Igbo while they make up this mythical story. Within this narration, Nri arrogates to himself this priestly character, anchoring his credibility on Chukwu. However, what interest us are this God-dimension and the fact that everything existing proceeds from him.

For the Delta Group, the world is infinitesimal when compared to the enormity of God. Thus, like the Babylonians, they thought that God could not have created the world directly. He needed to create *Adum* who, in turn, created *Bantole* and *Kooloo*: the first man and woman of the human race. Through *Adum* then, God is accessible to created realities.

Pre-historic myths in Igbo culture indicate that God was present in Igbo thought pattern and that the Igbo went further to show that God stands as the uncaused cause of all things. It further establishes man's need of constant interaction with God and paves the way to the realm of God via a ritual link through sacrificial systems (Metuh, 1985, p. 40).

Furthermore, the Nri account had Nri sacrifice his first son and daughter before the food items were revealed to him by God. God caused these food items to grow on their graves in a significant manner. The sacrifice made of the first son and daughter by Nri represents self-violence in dealing with famine. Their burial connoted a violence done to the earth so that subsequent food items may emerge from it. The whole picture represents a ritual that becomes the means by which the Igbo (human) breaks through the boundaries of the immanent to the transcendent. By obedience to the demands of *Chukwu*, Nri draws divine favours to himself; by sacrificing his most cherished possessions, he appropriates authority over *Ala* (the earth, both as a physical object and as a deity). Thus, Nri is at peace with *Igwe*—the abode of *Chukwu* and *Ala*, the fertility deity and the female counterpart of *Igwe*. While the Jewish God supplied a lamb in place of Isaac, whom he demanded as a sacrifice from Abraham—the progenitor of the Jewish race—, the Igbo God did not. Rather, he accepted the sacrifice of Nri and through it established a covenant between Nri and *Ala*—a covenant which all his progenies shall become parts of.

Chapter Fourteen

God-Indwelt Igbo Universe

A hermeneutics of the pre-historic excursus above will give us the proper understanding of Igbo world view. In discussing this world view, we must take two perspectives:

1. The Physical Universe
2. The Mystical Universe

The primal statement to be made here is that man is the ontological center or mean of the Igbo universe, be it physical or mystical. Igbo ontology is, therefore, basically anthropocentric. The same may be said about other African Traditional societies (Mbiti, 1975, p. 92). Consequently, God, deities, spirits, and spirit forces exist precisely for man. The *raison d'etre* of their being may not go beyond serving the purpose of man's welfare. The Igbo's is one world of dualized existence. Man lives in either of the modes of existence; what is important is that he goes on living.

The Physical Universe

Ifesieh (1989) gives an elaboration of Igbo view of the physical universe, which he opines is divided into two.

1. *The Celestial/Semi-Celestial.* This sphere is referred to as *Igwe* ('the sky'). It includes other physical entities like *Kpakpando* ('star'), *Anyanwụ* ('sun'), *Ọnwa* ('moon'), *Urukpu* ('cloud'), *Ogwurugwu* ('rainbow'), *Egbeigwe* ('thunder'), *Amụma* ('lightning'), *Ikuku* ('air'), *Ihe* ('light'), *Ọchịchịị* ('darkness'), and so forth. *Igwe* is the abode of God and some pure spirits. The physical entities as mentioned above associated with *Igwe* are viewed as divine manifestations. God, directly or indirectly, created the world and man besides. The celestial bodies and spirits are his emissaries and representatives. In the physical universe, there is a vertical distance separating god and the pure spirits above from the other side of the world—below. Although the Igbo are aware of this sphere, it does not at the same time pose any threat to him. The dynamism of the sphere is totally beyond his comprehension, and because this dynamism does not affect him directly, he seems to be more attentive to the intermediary, familiar, and ancestral spirits in his abode.

2. *The Terrestrial Sphere.* The earth is referred to as *Ala*—the abode of man and other animals and plants, especially those with religious significance and totemic relevance. *Ala* is *Igwe*'s female counterpart and a deity in its own right. It has custody of morality and dispenses fertility. Man is the king of this sphere and, in his kingship, takes on the duty of a moral vanguard in the name of *Eze/Di/Ọkpara*. It should be noted that *Eze* in Igbo society is not merely 'king' in the sense of Western or Eastern monarchies, but 'he who

excels.' *Eze* is a title given to one who excels in an industry. The Igbo makes an industry of any little aspect of life and conscientiously struggles to exercise an unchallengeable influence wherever he finds himself. He knows that in so doing he becomes an *Eze*—the highest title/qulification in the Igbo world of egalitarian specialization, like a Ph.D. Even the so-called traditional ruler was understood, before the imposition of the idea of monarchy by the British, as a custodian of ancestral objects and ethics; he excels in the wisdom of the ancients, which he basically understands as an industry, whereas his possible successor is gradually being trained in the anthologies of this same Sophia. *Eze*, *Di*, *Okpara*, and so forth are such titles in the Igbo culture that could better be rendered as 'adept' or 'master.' The meaning entails the quality of concretely excelling in an art. Finally, the physical world is understood as a vertical apartness. In this vertical apartness, there is no possibility of direct interaction between the two worlds. The only area open to man is the mystical way. *Ichuaja* is the practical exercise or ritualization of this mysticism.

The Mystical Universe

In this perspective, the Igbo universe is God indwelt. It is a single universe co-habited by men, God, and spirits alike. In an attempt to describe this universe, Metuh (1985) wrote: "Generally, the world of human experience is seen as one fluid coherent unit in which spirits, men, animals, plants and elements are engaged in continuous interaction" (p. 38) Nevertheless, the Supreme God—*Obinigwe*—rendered in contemporary language as *Chineke* or *Chukwu*—has severed direct communion with men as is evident in our analysis of the myth of origins. This severance in the experience of the Igbo seems irreversible. Consequently, the Igbo live content in the mystical world peopled by men and spirits—agents of *Obinigwe*—whose influence on men is enough preoccupation for the Igbo religious spirit. However, the mode of the relationship between these spirits, deities, disembodied spirits (ancestors), and *Obinigwe* is not clear to the average Igbo mind. Metuh (1985) opined,

> The Igbo recognize some relationship between Chukwu and deities. But their conception of this relationship is not very clear. God created the deities. But Igbo theology and mythology are not clear on why and how it came about. The deities are sometimes referred to as sons of Chukwu, or his messengers, and sometimes as his manifestations. (p. 38)

The Arụsi manifestations of Obinigwe are simply a demonstration of the Igbo belief in a God who shares this worldly concourse. God, in Igbo understanding, is not distant, abstract, or removed, neither is it limited to materiality and visibility. The mystical distance between the Igbo and God may be a hair's breath, felt rather in mediums. Unlike the Olympian gods, the Igbo God and the deities do not engage in wars, petty jealousies, immoral acts, and dubiety, nor are they held within the wheels of inexorable fatalism. Even the menacing spirits of the Igbo world that Christian thought has identified as evil were not categorized as such because whatever roles they played in the world of men were necessary for man's continued existence in this cohabited universe. Metuh (1981) had observed that it is "easy to see that the Igbo concept of evil spirits does not include the idea of moral evil... . Igbo evil spirits do not incite people to immoral deeds but bring them misfortunes" (p. 105).

In Igbo mysticism, evident in its mythology, as in the Jewish kabala, these so-called evil spirits are part of God. This rather negative side of God manifests when man, by some misconduct, falls short of the favour of God and the spirits.

The vagaries and vicissitudes of Igbo life bear witness to the operations of these menacing spirits, and the Igbo do not identify them as adversaries of God but complementary parts of him to keep man in check. This conceptualization explains why, in the sacrificial system of the Igbo, God, the deities, and bad spirits alike are beneficiaries without fear of contradiction. These form indispensable parts of the mystical universe. Even the numerous *Aruusi* manifestations are mutually inclusive in this universe. The votary of ITR is free to interact with as many as demand his obeisance without incurring the wrath of another, unlike the God of Judeo-Christian belief that, in His jealousy, may not bear contending with any other god. Evidently, the Igbo have not assimilated the idea of contradiction in appealing to different deities, even in their Christian profession. Ejizu (1992) observed,

> The indigenous world-view is essentially an integrated holistic and dynamic one in which the two oracles of reality—visible and invisible, the human world and the spiritual world—are believed to be intricately interrelated and intensely influence one another. There are no sharp lines of distinction between the sacred and profane. (p. 17)

The mystical Igbo universe presents the spirit abode as existing within this terrestrial linearity, that is, beyond linear horizon. (*Horizon* here must be understood as horizontal extension.) For instance, when one walks beyond seven rivers and seven forests, one bursts into the territories of the spirits. The yonder world of spirits is beyond the Igbo horizon measured in linear extension. Though adepts and masters understand the symbological implications of this statement, the truth is presented to the average and practical Igbo mind as it appears here.

Chapter Fifteen

Harmonious Concourse
of the Two Igbo World Orders

The mystical world of the Igbo is one, united, all-encompassing whole in which varieties of spirits, men, animals, trees, and inanimate objects coexist. Every component of this whole is as important as the other in as much as it serves the need of man who is the ontological center of this whole. God is the coordinating or galvanizing center of these divergent components or the principle of ontological unity in the universe. The Igbo seeks God solely for optimizing this unifying convergence.

Evidently, there had existed a primordial harmony and interaction between the two Igbo world orders in the mythical past. The Igbo saying "*Mgbe elu bu ala ọsa*" (when squirrels walked in the air as on ground) or "*Mgbe ezi dị n'ukwu ụkwa*" (when there was thoroughfare beside the breadfruit tree), they imply there was a time when there was an unmitigated harmony in the world among everything that is—God, deities, spirits, man, animals, plants, and so forth. The Igbo seem to portray primordial paradise. But this past most certainly is described in myths like fairy tales or *Alice in Wonderland*. In this mythical past, animals communicated with men, trees walked and even talked, spirits were visible, and so forth. Even then, the harmony and interaction was for the welfare of man. In as much as this harmony belongs to his mythical past, the Igbo had never out-lived the vacuum created by a possible disharmony and severance from the yonder world. Thus, the sacrificial systems are ritual means by which the Igbo ensure that harmony and interaction between the two world orders are sustained. Varied as its elements may be, Igbo sacrificial systems—like those of the Jews—are so rich in ritual significance that no aspect of the Igbo life is left unrepresented. The dominant significance of these elements is that they open up the spiritual area for man who otherwise has fallen out of favour with God and the spirits and make this area penetrable for man's exploits.

More than the Jewish Cabbalist, the Igbo demonstrates even in rituals that "evil" spirits (in ITR, best described by Arinze (1970) as "capricious and indignant spirits") are a necessary part of the Supreme Personality of Godhead, better described as His agents. They are not adversaries of God, privations, or the other negative polar region opposed to God. Like every other spirit, they are beneficiaries to man's sacrifice. *Ịchụaja* is the particular element of the sacrificial system that proves the case in point. Arinze, given his Christian background, understood the evil spirits as forces outside and opposed to God, and we think this is an unfair Christian imposition on ITR. Its far-reaching implication is that the Igbo are not sure of the force he is appealing to in a dual world order.

We have already seen that the Igbo's is a single world, peopled by varieties of spirits, men, animals, and inanimate things. The Supreme God, whose extreme awesomeness is terribly radicalized, scarcely has need of man's sacrifice. The Igbo has enough spiritual enterprise interacting with agent spirits but is never oblivious to the fact that they, after all, are God's emissaries. The Judeo-Christian jealous God does not allow for homage to even to an inferior, but the God of ITR is an image of contentment, competing with none other, never threatened by any power. M. Okpalaonyido (Personal Communication, April 24, 2006) said: *"Chukwu kere agwu kee Ekwensu ma gbanaha ha ka onye ọbụna n'ime ha kparaba ọnụ ya."* (God created the *capricious and indignant* spirits; in as much as he made himself inaccessible to them, it was that they too might be fed.) By inaccessibility, Okpalaonyido simply meant to imply that God was beyond the menacing pranks of such spirits. He was not asserting that they are adversaries of God or that the area of God is absolutely locked up to them. He meant also to show that God Himself was in agreement with the activities in the world of men through which they are fed. As God, He receives loyalties and homage from them. The Igbo, in a practical way, finds accommodation for all manner of spirits. At one time, it may seem to the external observer that the sacrificial (ritual) expression is to scare away the evil spirits, but at another time, the Igbo is seen as either placating or pacifying them because he also invokes them to action when he is in need of their power. In his religion, the Igbo incorporate practically everything, harmonizing them in a concordant relationship for the peace of man. The harmonious concourse of the Igbo two world orders is, therefore, a dialectical reality. The good and the evil, favourable and unfavourable, benevolent and malevolent spirits and forces are always in the necessary conflict of bringing this harmony about. *Ichụaja* is a means through which this dialectic could periodically be brought to a zero point on its continuum.

PART FIVE

ĮCHŲAJA IN THE TAXONOMY OF
RITUAL ELEMENTS IN
IGBO TRADITIONAL RELIGION

Chapter Sixteen

The Importance of Taxonomy
in the Study of Elements of Religion

Taxonomy is the science of classification used by the biological sciences, especially botany. The Swedish botanist, Carolus Linnaeus, had done the classification of plants based on natural relations in the 18th century, but its progressive influence has continued into this century. Bringing the relevance of this science to bear upon the study of religion, Ekunife (1990) has observed that:

> Classification facilitates insight into various ranges
> of ritual units of the topic under consideration. It is
> an important technique for exposing, comparing and
> testing hypothesis relating to empirical realities. It is
> also a means of generalizing from an accumulated
> data of field-work research. (p. 28)

Ịchụaja is not a new area to be explored in ITR, and it will not be an easy task to disagree on some points that have already been established. Because the field work did not include very many people, efforts were made to cover from east to west and north to south of the Igbo speaking area. Phonological and syntactic comparisons of *Ịchụaja* were presented in Chapter Twelve. The classifications in this chapter will help us to do some semantic and morphological comparisons in order to authenticate our claims. In our entire search, it is worth noting that there is no single Igbo word, already existing in the religious system, which could be used to translate *sacrifice* in its Christian garb unless the sacrificial theory upon which *Ịchụaja* could be grounded is found.

This conclusion could be in line with that of Arinze (1970), which we have tried to affirm and support; however, his work lacked a conceptual analysis of the word *Ịchụaja* which would have clarified this theory. The other ancient religions—Judaism and the Vedic Religions—may also have this problem. The truth is that different cultic rituals performed at different times and places and for different purposes have names given to them in all religions. Christianity especially of the Western cast, in its peculiar monotheistic idea—the one, only, ultimate, and consumatory incarnation or manifestation of God in Christ—began by rendering impotent, empty, and useless all former cult rituals, especially in Judaism, which gave it birth. The same Christianity did nothing to strip man of the need of all those rituals but posed to have replaced, transcended, and fulfilled them in Christ's sacrifice. The death of Christ became one single event that sufficed for all the former rituals. In the language of the Catholic Church, this act as a cult ritual is rendered *sacrificium*. We have tried to trace its etymology earlier and came to the conclusion that its principal character is immolation and oblation because the former would be lacking in religious value without the latter.

In Igbo Christianity, *Aja* has become conventionally accepted as sacrifice. In our taxonomical analysis, we address five elements in Igbo cultic ritual systems including *Įchụaja*, in the hopes of achieving three things:

1. To expose the semantic similarities or dissimilarities of the chosen elements in some Igbo subdivisions.

2. To delineate *Įchụaja* as an element and state its status among all other elements to ascertain its suitability for translating *sacrifice*.

3. To categorize the cultic elements in a clearer fashion, possibly employing new words to help us do so without contradicting anything in the religious system.

Chapter Seventeen

Taxonomy of Ritual Elements
in Igbo Religious Culture

The vast idea compressed in the Christian understanding of the word *sacrifice* has led many scholars to opine that no singular word translates *sacrifice* in ITR. The domination of Christianity for many centuries has put it in the forefront, especially in Western education. Our labour in this work is simply because our minds have been formed by this Christian idea of sacrifice as a standard; otherwise, the various ritual performances that we have subsumed under sacrificial systems each in its own right exhausts what it signifies. Those elements are simply the ones we consider fitting in the boundaries of the Christian idea of sacrifice. There still exist many elements in the religion, and true to its nature, many more are evolving. However, it is clear that the sacrifice of Christ and, therefore, sacrifice itself contains the totality of the Christian kerygma, whereas *Ịchụaja* which we are distinguishing as the constant high point in ITR is the center around which all other elements of the religion revolve and is a veritable tool to understanding the Igbo world-view. Nevertheless, representation of the various ritual elements in ITR will give an insight into the proper understanding of the elements to help sharpen our idea of *sacrifice* and so as to ascertain its equivalent in contemporary religious languages. The following tables display semantic comparisons of the various elements of ITR as seen in different areas of Igbo culture. Table 5 presents such information for the words referring to worship and adoration.

Table 5
Words Concerning Worship and Adoration in Some Subdivisions in Igbo Culture

Area	Town	Verb	Action
Northern Igbo	Obukpa	Ịgọmaa	Contenting or placating the spirits
Inland East Igbo	Ogwa	Ịgọmmụọ	Contenting the spirits
South Central Igbo	Akokwa	Imemmụọ	Celebrating the spirits
North Central Igbo	Akpo	Ịrọmmụọ	Celebrating the spirits
Southern Igbo	Amannachi	Ịrọmmụọ	Celebrating the spirits
Western Igbo	Asaba	Ịlọmmụọ	Celebrating the spirit

Worship or adoration of objects in ITR is a celebration, sometimes including carnivals, as described earlier in this work. The celebration is as religious as it is social. It is important to note that the verbs *Igọ*, *Ime*, and *Ịrọ/Ịlọ* could connote the activities of worship, veneration, and adoration, depending on the cultural area under review. This idea would be foreign to Basden (1966), who divided Igbo sacrifice into two—*Ịlọmmụọ* and *Ịgọmmụọ*— and interpreted the word *Ịgọ* as meaning 'to deny.' Nevertheless, the contemporary central *Igbo Izugbe* might say *Ife* or *Ịkpọisiala* ('to worship') or *Ịkpọku* or *Ibeku* ('to invoke'), but in this exercise, the dialects needed to be explored. The activities referred to in Table 5 offer contentment to the spirits and communion for humans. Table

6 displays semantic comparisons of the elements of ITR concerning expiation and purification.

Table 6
Words Concerning Expiation and Purification in Some Subdivisions in Igbo Culture

Area	Town	Verb	Action
Northern Igbo	Obukpa	Ịgọmaa	Invoking/placating the spirits
Inland East Igbo	Ogwa	Ịkwụarọ	To purify by dragging victim
South Central Igbo	Akokwa	Ịkwụala	To expiate by dragging on the earth
North Central Igbo	Akpo	Ịkwụarọ	To purify by dragging victim
Southern Igbo	Amannachi	Ịkwụala	To expiate by dragging on the earth
Western Igbo	Asaba	Ịkpụalọ	To purify by dragging victim

Ultimately it is the land (*Ala/Ana/Anị*) that is violated when a taboo is broken. *Ịkwụ/Ịkpụ* means 'to drag'; 'dragging' which is consistent in the variations here indicates the principal action in the liturgy of purification. *Ịkwụala* would literally mean 'dragging the earth,' but it is the animal or victim which is dragged on the face of the earth to cleanse it. The sense is that the victim carries with it the sin and its concomitant calamity and is dragged to death. There are other forms of purification in ITR, like Ịsaifi, with different liturgies. The words *Ikpocha/Ikwocha*, *Ịwụcha*, or *Ịzacha* might be preferable to today's Igbo. Even Christian Pastors have their own contemporary version called *Mkpocha na Nzacha*, that is informed by this traditional practice. Table 7 displays semantic comparisons of the elements of ITR referring to veneration and reverence.

Table 7

Words Concerning Veneration and Reverence in Some Subdivisions in Igbo Culture

Area	Town	Verb	Action
Northern Igbo	Obukpa	Ihunru	To pay homage
		Ịtọrọ maa ihe	Dedicating something to the spirit
Inland East Igbo	Ogwa	Ihunru	To pay homage
South Central Igbo	Akokwa	Ihummụọ	Paying homage or loyalty to the spirits
North Central Igbo	Akpo	Ifenhu	Paying homage or loyalty
Southern Igbo	Amannachi	Ihuala	Loyalty to the earth
Western Igbo	Asaba	Irunru	To pay homage

Veneration or reverence is principally focused on the spirits, deities, or ancestors, among whom is *Ala*, the Earth, as can be seen in Amannachi. We also encountered varieties like *Ihueke* and *Ihuogwugwu* using the names of specific deities. However, veneration has its social dimension, focused on human beings due to status, patriotism, philanthropy, or for some remote spiritual reasons. To whomsoever homage is done, it requires a significant or symbolic object, whatever it may be. In some instances, veneration and reverence could be understood as paying homage or loyalty. *Ife* is more contemporary than *Ihu/Iru*. However, all are still in use in today's Igbo. *Nru/Nhu* is veneration or reverence. *Ihunru/Ihunhu/Irunru* is one of those Igbo words that combine the verb and noun together for emphasis. We can see others like *Ipempe* ('being small'), *Ịsọnsọ* ('being in a state of ritual purity'), *Igbamgba* ('wrestling'), *Ịrọnrọ* ('dreaming dream'), and so forth. The words could be described as tautaulogical truisms. Table 8 displays semantic comparisons of the elements of ITR referring to sacrifice.

Table 8

Words Concerning Sacrifice in Some Subdivisions in Igbo Culture

Area	Town	Verb	Action
Northern Igbo	Obukpa	Ịchụaja Igbuaja	To slay a victim
Inland East Igbo	Ogwa	Ịchụaja	To slay a victim
South Central Igbo	Akokwa	Ịchụaja Ịsụaja	To slay a victim
North Central Igbo	Akpo	Ịchụaja	To slay a victim
Southern Igbo	Amannachi	Ịchụaja	To slay a victim
Western Igbo	Asaba	Ịchụaja	To slay a victim

Ịchụaja/Igbuaja/Ịsụaja is a derivations from the very action that signifies this ritual element of ITR. This action is basically the immolation of a victim in its various renditions. Our informants have demonstrated that there is a moment of *Ịchụaja* in all ritual practices of ITR, and at that moment, the victim is slain. In addition, the prefixes *Igbu* and *Ịsụ* give us a further clue to this claim, considering their root in the cultural area where they are used. This exercise was elaborated upon in Chapter Twelve. The essence is to shed blood and subdue, symbolizing human submission to divine will and denouncement of initial human revolt. *Ịchụaja* is the Igbo word that comes closest to translating as *sacrifice*. Indeed, it exactly translates as *sacrifice* when both words are considered etymologically. *Ịchụaja* is a holy and practical act in ITR, performed with a great deal of reverence. Table 9 presents semantic comparisons of the elements of ITR referring to conjuration and invocation.

Table 9

Words Concerning Conjuration and Invocation in Some
Subdivisions in Igbo Culture

Area	Town	Verb	Action
Northern Igbo	Obukpa	Ịgọọhọ	Invoking the blessing/power of ọhọ
Inland East Igbo	Ogwa	Ihuọfọ	Conjuring or Invoking ọfọ (together with the spirit of uprightness and justice)
South Central Igbo	Akokwa	Ịgọọfọ	Invoking the blessing/power of ọfọ
North Central Igbo	Akpo	Ịgọọvwọ/ Iboọvwọ	Invoking or superimposing the power/blessing of ọvwo
Southern Igbo	Amannachi	Ịgọọfọ	Invoking the blessing/power of ọfọ
Western Igbo	Asaba	Ịgọọvọ	Invoking the blessing/power of ọfọ

Ọfọ, ọvọ, ọvwọ, or *ọhọ* is normally identified as a symbol of justice (represented by wood cut from the plant *detarium Senegalense/elastica*). Though it is a stem, it is an object that bears within it reality of the spirits of great ancestors. As an ancestral symbol, the Ọfọ can also be conjured and invoked. The object is wrought with enormous spiritual powers and cannot be borne in the hands of a man lacking in moral rectitude. Its effect on a person who fails its criterion is always decisive and devastating. Ọfọ is recharged from time to time and called *Ịgwọke* or *Ịgwake Ọfọ.* The process of *Iwube* ('instituting') or *Ịgwọke* ('re-energizing') Ọfọ always includes *Ịchụaja.* Even the momentary or daily *Ịgọ/Ịbọ/Ihu* ('conjuring' or 'invoking') *Ọfọ* requires *Ịchụaja,* which could be in the forms of libation, spitting munched kola, or even slaying a chicken and smearing it with its blood.

This exercise in taxonomy clarifies that it is not just a problem of nomenclature posed by the study of cultic rituals in ITR. The concepts, while common, either vary or conflict in name and in liturgy. For instance, what the Akpo people of North Central Igbo call *Irommuo*, the Ogwa people of Inland East Igbo call *Igommuo*. These two concepts were distinguishing for Basden (1966) in the sacrificial system, but we have learnt that, varied as the concepts may be, they connote one and the same thing for different people.

Chapter Eighteen

Resolving Possible Problems
from the Taxonomy

In the previous chapter, we undertook the taxonomy of five cultic rituals: Ịgọmmụọ (Ịrọmmụọ), Ịkpụarụ, Ihunru, Ịgọọfọ, and Ịchụaja. The taxonomy presented a seemingly confusing array of rituals, especially with the verb that should give us the controlling meaning of the concepts. At this juncture, we agree with Metuh (1985) that the verb will help us distinguish the idea of the cultic ritual of our study. However, unlike Metuh, we need to further explore and manipulate the concepts to gather from them as much meaning as possible.

We agree with Arinze (1970) that the objects of ITR are God, spirits, deities, and ancestors. These we called *Obinigwe (Ezelu), Mmụọ, Arụsị*, and *Ndịichie*. Any of these may be a beneficiary of an ITR cultic ritual in accordance with the stipulations of *Afa*. Furthermore, these objects can go by the generic name *Mmuo*, which derives from the two dimensions of the Igbo world *Bemmadụ/ Alammadụ* and *Bemmụọ/Alammụọ*. To *Bemmadụ/Alammadụ*, belong man and all physical entities. To *Bemmụọ/Alammụọ*, belong all spiritual entities: *Obinigwe* (*Ezelu*), *Mmuo*, and *Ndiichie*. *Aruso* essentially belongs to *Bemmuo/Alammuo*, but it is localized in groves and shrines, though it is worth mentioning that, as spirits, they cannot be confined within that terrestrial area. Consequently, they operate beyond their demarcated boundaries and may from time to time desert the shrine depending on factors. *Arusi* is *Mmuo*. The Northern Igbo, especially in the Nsukka area, understand the extreme implication of this statement so much that what the Southern Igbo call *Arusi*, they call *Maa* (*Mmuo*). In this analysis, we reduce the object of ITR to *Mmuo*. *Mmuo* in its various presentations is the beneficiary of the cultic rituals. With this, Metuh's idea, that it is the verb that distinguishes one ritual from another, makes sense. We emphasize that whether it is *Obinigwe*, *Mmuo*, *Arusi*, or *Ndiichie*, the multidimensional object of ITR is *MMUO*. *Mmuo* is One in Many and Many in One.

Based on this analysis, we distinguish four major elements in Igbo cultic systems: *Irummuo*, *Igommuo*, *Irommuo*, and *Imedommuo*. Within these four elements could be subsumed others we had earlier discussed in this study. Meanwhile, the verbs *iru*, *igo*, *iro*, and *imedo* are the varying but controlling verbs that we will use to distinguish one element from another.

Irummuo

The word *irummuo* implies veneration of and reverence to the spirits. Other variables of the word include irunru, *ifenru*, *ihunru*, *ifenhu*, and *ihunhu*, all meaning the same thing. *Irummuo* also includes all other nuances of attaching the name of a deity or spirit personage to the controlling verb *iru*, *ihu* or *ife* – *iruano* (venerating or reverencing *ani*), *iruchukwu* (venerating or reverencing *Chukwu*), *irueze* (venerating or reverencing the adept), and so forth.

Arinze (1970) described this element thus: "The iru Ani ceremony, the animal sacrifice to the ani of Onitsha performed by the Obi through a person representing him is for the welfare of all Onitsha people and is solemn" (p. 39). *Irummụọ* belongs to the category of *Ajanchụnye*. It also includes *iruọfọ, iruchi, iruajana*, and so forth. In any of the cases, it is a communal solemn celebration with or without carnival. The ceremony contains *Ịchụaja*, which features oblation, immolation, and communion. Even when this veneration or reverence is done to a human being, it has a religious undertone.

Ịgommụọ

The word *Ịgommụọ* literally means 'invocation' and 'conjuration.' The Igbo invoke or conjure spiritual powers in various situations: in preparation for a funeral, for protection, for general welfare, and so forth. It is done when one is sure that he is at rights with the spirits. If one's hands are soiled for whatever reason, the spirits cannot come to his aid. Basden (1966) observed that:

> The petitioner asserts that he has done no wrong; he has not trespassed against the law of the land, or against the community, then why has this evil befallen him? If, however, by any chance he has sinned inadvertently, he now makes this sacrifice as atonement for these unknown misdeeds …. A man who knows perfectly well that he is guilty of wrongdoing will, on no account, venture to make sacrifice to the "igo-maw". He would be in mortal dread lest the spirit should take summary vengeance on his hypocrisy. (p. 56)

The Nsukka region of Northern Igbo also refers to this as *Ịkpọmaa*. *Ịgọmmụọ* includes elements like *Ajaezelu* (also known as *Anyanwụnaezelu* or *Anyanwụnaagbala*). There is also *Ịtụegbo* (or *Ịtụemo*) and *Ịgọ/Ibọọfọ*. Before the funeral of a dignitary—*Onye chizuru echizu*—and who is in good standing before the people, there must be *Ịtụegbo* because the funeral is going to attract a variety of people from far and near. It is also done during large festivals that are envisaged to attract varieties of people. Such funerals and festivals are celebrated with great pomp. *Ịtụegbo* is done basically to fortify the area of the event from evil attack and even evil intent. Umeh (1997) indicated, "*Odaghini-Okwalu* [were] mystical divine brakes that kept all in their places and prevented them from falling into oblivion" (p. 7) and a major part in *Ịtụegbo*. Earlier, he had described *Ọdaghịnị-Ọkwalọ* as:

> Igbo version of magnetic fields and balances involving also the mystical brakes that prevented all these planets, satellites, stars and other heavenly bodies from crashing into each other and from falling into "ikelekwum mmuo" (spiritual fathomless abyss). (pp. 4-5)

Umeh was, however, describing the origin of the world as *ụwa walụ awa*—a kind of Big-Bang and asserted *Ọdaghịnị-Ọkwalụ* as the agent of stability and balance in the chaotic bang.

Outside this understanding, *Ọdaghịnị-Ọkwalụ* is also a kind of concoction known to the *dibịa* alone and used in *Ịtụegbo*. Umeh (1997) was not at ease giving the elaborate ritual activity of *Ịtụegbo*, though he recorded that:

> Two tree posts made of *Ogilisi* and *Asusu-aka*, or similar sacred trees, are erected and some palm fronds

and yellow leaves are ritually tied and adorned with mystical symbols and put across, resting on the two tree posts. (p. 7)

Okonkwo (Personal Communication, April 5, 2006) also indicated these other items used for Ituegbo:

1. *Ji* (Yam)
2. *Okeokpa* (a Cockerel)
3. *Igu Nkwu* (Palm Frond)
4. *Akwukwo ohia* (Herbs) – *akoro, Obuegbe, onunkwo* and so forth

O. Okonkwo (Personal Communication, April 5, 2006) of Okwurokwu in Amannachi Orsu Local Government Area of Imo State deliberately withheld the names of some of the herbs used in *Ituegbo*. This is one of the characters of the *dibia* – ability to keep secret some of their practices

The *Ogilisi* stems as posts are mounted at the appropriate places. The fowl is slain (*Ichuaja*); the yam sliced. The herbs and yam slices are tied within the palm frond and the blood of the fowl smeared on the wrap. Then, the wrapping is done, twisting the leaves of the palm frond in an artistic manner to make a long bunch, and the bunch is adorned with sacred symbols, which Umeh (1997, p. 7) suggested could be *Egbeku Ukpaka* (circular shell of *Ukpaka* pod), *Nku* (Rectangular or square fan, a day old chick), and/or *Ogbalandu* (a special creeping stem used as tying rope). The whole bunch is hung across the *Ogilisi* posts, which serves as the main entrance of the arena, or lay on the ground between the posts. It is believed that anything evil that crosses it shall be met with a summary vengeance. These include harmful charms, concoctions, or poison, or even an ill-willed or evil-intentioned fellow may not cross the *Egbo* without suffering a terrible calamity.

The priest goes out after the conjuration without a word, and nobody talks to him on his way back. Meanwhile, he goes home with the carcass of the fowl. Sometimes, *Egbo* is placed across the posts both above and below. Furthermore, *Egbo* can be of many types: *Egbo onwuike* (for preventing sudden deaths), *Egbo Ọria Ofufe* (for prevention of communicable diseases), *Egbo Ọ biara egbu m* (for returning harmful forces directed against one to the sender. In today's colloquial language, it is called 'Back-to-sender'), and so forth. In my clan, there is a legendary *Egbo* that was done across the main entrance to the area of settlement of my people in 1918. It was said that, because of it, no person died in our clan during the influenza pandemic. It is still within living memory that it was only our clan that did not lose a soul during the whole period of the attack in the whole community. It is also within living memory that the *Egbo* done during the funeral of Ezenwata Ezenwamma of Umuezechineke clan in Amaife village, Akpo, trapped, neutralized, and turned back a harmful masquerade from Adazi-Nnukwu in Aniocha Local Government Area of the same state.

Igọmmụọ includes also *Idoiyi/Ịtụiyi*—a charm done to protect properties from external invasion, one of which is called *Nome* in Abakaliki of Northern Igbo; *Igọọfọ*—invoking the spirit of the ancestors; *Ịkwaiyi*—summoning one to an oath or placing a curse on one especially in disputes. Some use *Ọfọ* (the ancestral symbol of justice and uprightness) and in some cases *Arụsị*—a deity—for this purpose; *Ịtụarụsị*—the invocation of a deity for assistance. The recent and so moch trumpeted secret rituals of Ogwugwu in okija are a case in point about *Ịtụarụsị*. Politicians were reported to have gone to this shrine to make covenanats and oaths to bind themselves in trustful collaboration and reassure themselves of faithful allegiance to their political bargains. Many have appealed to the deity as the supreme judge of cases whose draconian verdict could be summoned until the recent calamity that befell it. However, its influence has not been totally abated.

Irommụọ/Ịlọmmụọ

This word literally means 'worshipping, celebrating, or adoring the spirits.' The form of this word has been described in Chapter Ten under the subtitle "*Ajanchụnye.*" It is communitarian in nature and often is accompanied by carnivals as discussed previously.

This literally means 'appeasement and placation.' It includes all expiatory sacrifices *Ịkpụalụ*, *Ịchụogbunuke*, *Isaifi*, and so forth. It is the core element of *Ajanchụpụ* and contains what Arinze (1970) and Metuh (1985) referred to as *Ịchụaja*, as the sole element in its liturgy. The Northern Igbo alluding to this same concept uses a more apt word, *Igbuaja*, which places one in no doubt about the nature of the concept: immolation. *Immedommụọ* could also be rendered *Imerịammụọ*.

A diagrammatic representation of these elements in Igbo cultic ritual is displayed in Figure 2.

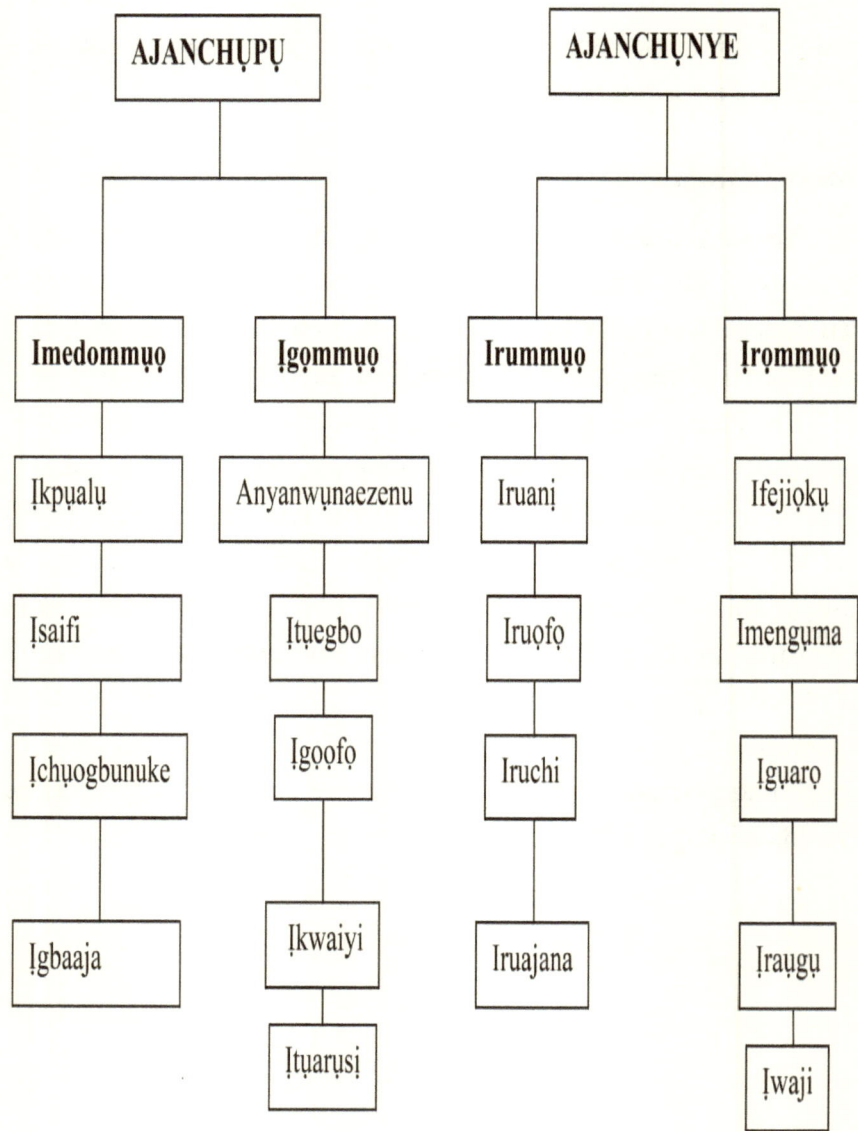

Figure 2. Diagramatic representation of the divisions of Igbo cultic rituals.

In keeping with our earlier analyses, there are four basic ritual elements in ITR: *Imedommụọ*, *Ịgọmmụọ*, *Irummụọ*, and *Ịrọmmụọ*. All other ritual elements whose list we cannot exhaust here both for want of space and the natural prolificity of such phenomenon in ITR fall under these four elements. *Ajanchụpụ* or *Ajanchụnye* is the mode of *Ịchụaja* required in the various and varied liturgies. *Ajanchụpụ* and *Ajanchụnye* which could have naturally appeared at the bottom of the table were deliberately placed at the top to allow for further increase of items in this list of ritual elements.

Chapter Nineteen

Comparative Analysis of the Different Perspectives
of *Ịchụaja* in Igbo Culture

Arinze (1970) admitted the idea of sacrifice on which he based his whole work: "We follow the authors of this last school. Therefore sacrifice is composed essentially of two elements: oblation and immolation. Oblation can be taken as the matter, immolation as the form of sacrifice" (p. 33). Nevertheless, Arinze also warned:

> The "something done" to the offered thing is called immolation. But this word need not bring blood at once before the mind. Immolation is according to the nature of the victim. Animals may be killed, liquids poured out, solids burnt. (pp. 32-33)

Arinze belonged to the school of Thomas Aquinas, which opined that it is immolation that determines, specifies, and reserves oblation to God alone. For this school, oblation and immolation are the two hinges upon which hang the doors of sacrifice. Yet the third aspect—communion—may not be entirely jettisoned. We are also in agreement with this school: Immolation and oblation are the principal characters of sacrifice.

We could also radicalize this thought by saying that immolation is the essential character of sacrifice because, by the nature of the sacrificial action, it presumes oblation. Communion may or may not take place. However, when it does, it emphasizes humanity's comformity to divine disposition to encompass it. This is beautifully demonstrated in the story of the Last Supper. Jesus' insistence on the ritual purity of His disciples drove Him to wash their feet in order that they may be worthy of that divine concourse. The Catholic Church also emphasizes the need for this ritual purity. In ITR, all nuances of *Ajanchụnye* that obviously include communion require ritual purity. Ritual purity is the form by which a votary could be presumed worthy of a divine contact. In this sacred meal, as it were, the human and the divine are in perfect union.

Sometimes Christianity tends to present sacrifice as empty cult ritualism. However, without the interior conformity of the votary, the exterior act of purification or even sacrifice is bereft of efficacy. Von Cochen (1996) underscores this amazing Catholic idea of sacrifice after the manner of the Council of Trent (1545-1563):

> The full and proper meaning of sacrifice is an offering
> of something external to ourselves to the most High
> God, consecrated or hallowed in a solemn manner by
> a lawfully appointed and duly qualified minister of
> the church, to recognize and testify to the supreme
> dominion of Almighty God over all creatures. (p. 1)

Sacrifice such as this is still in the mode of ignorance, borrowing from the idea of Vedic religions.

In principle, Christianity knows the idea of interior sacrifice and, in fact, admits of its animating role to the exterior act, but the idea of Christ, his centrality and finality, makes the votary's interior conformity to the external act of Christian sacrifice difficult. The Christian understands himself or herself as nothing while Christ is everything. There is always the tendency of projecting Christ while staying away from Him, but the idea of the interior disposition is being one with Him. For instance, a man tormented by evil spirits in offering the sacrifice of Christ for his safety does not appease or placate the tormenting spirit; he humiliates and subdues it with the power of Christ's sacrifice, himself hidden in Christ.

This idea presents a problem for the Igbo Christian because, outside the area of sacrifice, he is at difficulty keeping still in being concealed by Christ. When such a person tarries outside the vicinity of that sacrifice, he tends to expect a counter-attack from the evil spirits. In ITR, when a spirit menaces, the votary pays his ransom. Every menacing spirit qualifies for his sacrifice; he does not aim at expelling it, nor does he intimidate it. When he has paid his due, he is more likely to be confident that he does not owe. How may we Christianize this idea without contradicting the very core of the Christian message? One of our problems with Arinze (1970) is that he had already set for himself a Christian standard and was all along seeking the phenomenon in ITR that would comform to his standard. He was not perturbed by the enormity of challenges before him.

As discussed previously in Chapter Twelve, Metuh (1985) offered four perspectives on sacrifices: *Ịgọmmụọ*, *Imerịammụọ*, *Ịchụaja*, and *Ịkpụarụ*. Metuh also fell prey to the same distraction as Arinze (1970). We understand Metuh's divisions as ritual elements in ITR, but Metuh indicated divisions of sacrifice, so it would be dangerous to understand him as saying divisions of *Ịchụaja*.

Otherwise, it would be unusual for him to use the term *Ịchụaja*. We agree with Metuh on these perspectives because this division means that *Ịchụaja* is a perspective in the larger idea of sacrifice. Perhaps that is why he chose *Aja* as the translation of sacrifice and understood *Ịchụaja* as 'driving away evil spirits.' Thus, we have two perspectives—*Ajanchụpụ* and *Ajanchụnye*—as modes of *Ịchụaja* in all other ritual elements of ITR. *Ịchụaja* has two qualities: Oblation and Immolation. In the ritual elements requiring *Ajanchụpụ*, communion is not featured, but in *Ajanchụnye* communion is featured because the ritual elements requiring *Ajanchụnye* are communal in character and mystically reconciliatory.

PART SIX

ỊCHỤAJA
THROUGH THE PRISM OF
ORAL TRADITIONS
OF IGBO RELIGIOUS CULTURE

Chapter Twenty

Names

The elements of oral tradition that we employ in this part are names, proverbs, liturgies, myths, and folklore. These are truly the sources of ITR. We intend to situate *Ịchụaja* within their various contexts in our bid to expose the phenomenon to further evaluation. The warning we shall give at the beginning is that we have not yet come to a conclusion about the issue of *Ịchụaja*, so we are wary of translating it or whatever nuance in which it appears as 'Sacrifice'. In as much as it shall come to that, we do not strive to be there in a hurry. Nevertheless, for want of vocabulary, we shall employ the word *sacrifice* in translating either *Aja* or *Ịchụaja*, wherever they appear.

Names are very important in the study of African world-view. They contain religious and philosophical ideas of the African people. In Africa, names are not given arbitrarily; they are used to paint a picture of circumstances, portray situations, express wishes, and project expectations. Therefore, there are no Igbo names without a meaning. Basden (1966) observed that circumstances or prevailing conditions of the time, may suggest an appropriate name whereby the unusual happenings are kept in remembrance. Some of the names sound rather strangely to the European ears, for it should be remembered that all names are capable of translation. (p. 174)

Names are verifiable literary tools in oral literature because they are part of the means of preserving ideas. We shall do a hermeneutic analysis of four Igbo names that say something about Aja to help us grasp the hidden meaning of *Aja* in them.

Aja-Egboo-Ọnwụ. (Literarily: 'Sacrifice has prevented death.') Such a name may be given by a father who survived a possible death through his ritual offering of a ransom to the spirits. The name is meant to keep the memory of the experience alive. It could also have been the mother who survived the death, or the child itself may have been divined to be in mortal danger before birth. Whatever the case, the name is suggestive of a survival by means of sacrifice. The Igbo do not seek healing by drugs alone. According to Metuh (1985) "The Igbo distinguish between *dibia afa*, diviner, and *dibia ogwu*, medicine-man. Both are dibia (healers). However whereas, the one heals by afa, divination, the other heals by Ogwu, medicine" (p. 162). However, that may be, *Ọgwụ* which is often rendered as 'medicine' is at the same time magical, spiritual, and material. Though Metuh seemed to be deliberately inexhaustive on this matter, there is also the *Dibịaạja* in whom we are more interested. We have learnt already that *Aja* is subject to *Afa* in circumstances like this, so we presume *Aja* follows *Afa* even in Metuh's case. *Afa* might have demanded a ritual paying of ransom, which having been satisfied, an impending death was averted. Furthermore, the *Dibia* is not just a healer; he is "the knower, master or adept." The *Dibịa* is at the apex in the strata of knowledge in the Igbo religious world, each specializing in an area (*Afa*, *Aja*, or *Ọgwụ*).

However, there is a problem raised by another name: *Aja-egbo-ọnwụ*. This name implies that death cannot be averted by a ritual paying of ransom. Sometimes, Igbo thought is rife with such complexities. An external observer might see a contradiction in a matter like this and be put off from going further in his research. However, we say there is no contradiction. Ultimately, the Igbo understand that there is a supreme power that is unsurpassable in the universe and the wits of man cannot penetrate the totality of its secrets. Man's sacrifices are still subject to the discretion of this power. Nevertheless, the Igbo do not stop at anything to play their role in the universe for the saying goes, "*a gana achụ aja ka ikpe na-ama ndị mmụọ.*" (T—he necessary sacrifices should be made so that whatever goes wrong should be blamable on the spirits.) That is, in spite of the person fulfilling his religious obligation, the spirit might decide to do otherwise, but he may be adjudged as having done his best. In *Aja-egboo-ọnwụ*, the Igbo, even in extolling the efficacy of *Aja*, acknowledge (silently) the supreme role of the spirits who accepted it. Also in *Aja-egbo-ọnwụ*, the Igbo acknowledge man's role and accept the discretion of the spirits who are always in all circumstances final arbiters. The two variants could also be understood in the light of the religio-magico theory of Madu (2004). *Ajaegboo-ọnwọ* is the magical perspective of *Aja*, in which the Igbo asserts his ability to manipulate the spiritual entities. On the other hand, *Ajaegbo-ọnwụ* underscores the religious attitude of the Igbo in acknowledging the surpassing power of the spirits, in spite of man's efforts.

Ọnwụ-Asọ-Aja. (Literarily: 'Death does not stoop to sacrifice.') Death constitutes an irresolvable puzzle for the Igbo mind. The Igbo shows evidence of frustration in his encounter with the reality of death. Basden (1966) has this comment in that direction:

> The Ibo is somewhat a fatalist. This is perhaps, more obvious during illness than in other circumstances. If a patient get a notion that his complaint is of serious nature, it is more than probable that he will yield to despair and cease to struggle towards recovery; he is suffering from what has proved a fatal illness in the case of others: why contend against fate? So it often comes about that a patient dies for no other reason than he has not the will-power to live: to die is the appropriate thing to do! (p. 269)

Though Basden's comment here is outrageously negative and misleading, he captures an inherent attitude of the Igbo towards stopping death: he may seek metaphysical causes and not physical remedies. He does not give up until he achieves the aim of all his efforts but at the same time cultivates an open area of resignation if it is obvious that he is wrestling an unyielding spirit phenomenon. *Ọnwụ-asọ-anya* ('Death is not a respecter of persons'), *Ọnwụ-ama-nze* ('Death does not recognize the highly placed'), *Agbapụlụ-ọnwụ* ('Death is inescapable'), *Ezete-ọnwụ* ('Death is unavoidable'), *Ọnwụ-ka* ('Death is supreme'), and *Ọnwụzuruigbo* ('Death is universal'), among others, are some Igbo names that bring out the overwhelming nature of death. *Ọnwụ-asọ-aja*, like *Aja-egbo-ọnwụ*, is a lighter version compared to the ones stated above. Another rendition of *Ọnwụ-aso-aja* is *Ọnwụ-eri-aja* ('Death is not placable by sacrifice'). Death must come when it must come in spite of one's ritual paying of ransom.

Aja-Egbu-Edi. (Literarily: 'The disposed victim of a ritual exercise does not kill the wild cat.') The wild cat is a carnivorous animal that preys on smaller animals, especially chickens. It is always a menace to the domestic birds at night. These domestic birds are the commonest items used for *Ịchụaja*. *Aja*, especially of the brand of *Ajanchụpụ*, are placed at strategic places for tormenting spirits, whatever they may be. Thus, the Igbo think such oblation as dangerous to be tampered with, like eating the food of a hungry and angry fellow. The Igbo know that eventually such oblation that is placed in the open beside the bush, on crossroads, at shrines, or at river banks is vulnerable to preying animals that do, in fact, consume them, though there are also some human scavengers. The name rather underscores the malevolent nature of the spirit to whom *Aja* (in this circumstance) is offered. After all, the Igbo say, "*Tụpụrụ ndị mmụọ nni n'iro egborona ha ọgụ ha na nkịta.*" (Throw the food items to the spirits at the space [libation] do not be perturbed about their struggle with the dogs.) In other words, even the spirits know that the wild cat, like the dog or the vulture, is an agent in the consumption of *Aja*. Nonetheless, it is not with ease that they feed on the food set aside for the spirits. These prey are an important part of the whole exercise; after all, "*a chụọ aja ahụghị udene a mara n'ihe mere na be mmụọ.*" (When the victim for a sacrifice is slain, and there is no sign of preying vultures, then all is not well in the spirit abode.) This harmonious interaction between the offerer of sacrifice, the victim, the spirit to which sacrifice was offered, the sacred spot for the sacrifice, and the constant threat of the predator brings out beautifully the single world of the Igbo that admits in one whole all manner of beings and existence: an all-inclusive world.

Ọfọ-Ka-Aja. (Literarily: 'Uprightness is superior to sacrifice.') *Ọfọ* is a short wood cut from *detarium senegalense/elastica*. It is a symbolic object for uprightness and guilelessness. Basden (1966) remarked about *Ọfọ* that it is "sometimes referred to as the 'God of Justice.' The symbol is a stick cut from the ofo tree which becomes effective after consecration. All Igbo men, and a great many women, possess 'ofo'" (p. 57). *Ọfọ na ogu* is the fullness of guarantee for divine favours. *Iji ogu na ọfọ* means being in possession of the finest guarantee for divine favours superior to *Aja*. Perhaps this is the Igbo way of recasting the statement of Samuel: "Surely, to obey is better than sacrifice, and to heed than the fat of rams" (1Sam 15:22). In other words, uprightness is better than sacrifice. By extension or implication, the offering of sacrifice is not as important as the interior disposition of the offerer. Thus, this name brings forth the limitations of sacrifice. It is not the observable ritual but the internal disposition of the offerer that guarantees the efficacy of the sacrifice.

In all the names above, it should be noted that the word *Aja* was used in all circumstances and not *Ịchụaja*. Nevertheless, one could still say, "Ịchụaja egbo onwu" for *Aja-egbo-ọnwọ*, "Iji ọfọ ka ịchụ aja" for *Ọfọ-ka-aja*, and "Ọnwụ asọ ịchụaja" for *Ọnwụ-asọ-aja*, and still be correct. However, it is not uncommon in the Igbo country for names to be shortened for convenience. We see instances like *Nke dị n'iru ka mma* ('What lies in the future is always better') rendered as *Nkiru* or *Ngọzi Chukwu ka mma* ('God's blessing is the best') rendered as *Ngọzi* or *Ife ọma Chukwu mere* ('The good deed wrought by God') rendered as *Ifeọma*. If these names are taken in their shortened forms, the profundity of their meaning may be lost. On the one hand, *Aja* in the names we have analyzed could be a shortened form of *Ịchụaja*; on the other hand, it could just be *Aja*. We shall still specify the relationship between *Ichụaja* and *Aja*.

Chapter Twenty-one

Proverbs

Metuh (1985) rightly observed that "Proverbs are one of the most reliable forms of oral tradition, and as such are vehicles of the authentic beliefs of peoples living in preliterate societies" (p. 23). The Igbo say: "*Ilu bụ mmanụ e ji eri okwu.*" (Literarily: 'Proverbs are oil with which words are eaten.') Knowledge of proverbs in speeches is a good sign of wisdom. The Igbo regard anybody who exercises good command of proverbs as being close to the ancestors. When one tactically uses proverbs in one's speech, you may hear the Igbo say something like: "*Ọọ nna gị mụrụ gọ.*" (You are a true son of your father.) This is an encomium that gladdens the heart of the Igbo. One who uses proverbs with tact, precision, and fluency may be understood as endowed with ancient wisdom and can be called a repertoire of philosophy, history, and tradition. There are thousands of Igbo proverbs, and quite a number are being lost because of lack of literary records, interest, and motivation. Also, the various Igbo institutions and practices that generated them have been either seriously mutilated or completely exterminated. There are quite a number of proverbs that have to do with *Aja* and *Ịchụaja* in the Igbo culture. They give us clues to understanding the wisdom of the ancients about these words. We shall examine just a few of them.

Oke Dibia chụọ aja ọ di ka o nyere ndị mmụọ n'aka. (Literally: 'When a great priest sacrifices, it is like he handed the victim immediately to the spirits.') *Oke Dibia* is the adept who is in perfect contact with the spirits. He observes the taboos strictly and is ritually pure. In addition, he should be very knowledgeable in the appropriate rites of sacrifice and perform them with expertise effortlessly. To hand something immediately means that one is not in doubt whether it was received or whether such a thing reached its final destination because there is no mediacy. In performing his ritual, the *Oke Dibia* does not leave anybody in doubt; he fills everybody with satisfaction, joy, and confidence. He seems to have negotiated at par with the spirits. From this proverb, we learn that the *Dibịa* (in this instance) is a sacrificing priest and *mmụọ* is the religious object to which sacrifices are made.

Onye chi ya wara aja ehi, ya hụ nwa ọkụkọ, ya ekewere chi ya ekpe. (Literally: 'Whosoever his *chi* has asked a cow for a victim of sacrifice may offer a chicken and promise to make it up to his *chi* in his will.') The proverb confirms what we had already addressed in Chapter Nine: Our informants are agreed on the idea that *aja na-awa awa*. So *Afa* may pass the verdict that it is a cow that ones *chi* is demanding as victim. The chicken that one offers is a sign of goodwill and acceptance. Such a person hangs on the hope that someday he will make it up to his *chi*; otherwise, part of his will should include that the living make this sacrifice in his stead. The spirits are not as exacting as many authors have tried to portray them; they visit votaries in accordance with their state. When Arinze

(1970) wrote that the victim of *Ịchụaja* is "despicable," he did not seem to consider the possibility that the victim of *Ịchụaja* can be a wide variety of things, depending on the stipulations of *Afa* and that the verdict of *Afa* is not contestable. Such a person who offers a chicken surely cannot afford the cow at the material moment of its demand.

Ọbụrụ na ogbenye enweghi ihe ọ ga-eji chụrụ chi ya aja, o kwere chi ya ọnwụ. (Literarily: 'If a poor man does not have anything with which to sacrifice to his *chi*, he resigns to death.') The traditional Igbo society does not have a destitute class. Poverty is defined not by the lack of money or material possessions, estate, or property but by the strength of relations with others. Some have described the Igbo word for 'the poor,' *Ogbenye*, as being a compressed version of *ogbe na-enye*, which literarily means 'the village supplies,' implying that the poor is anyone for whom the community supplies. Whether this statement is true or not is not really important, in as much as it is true that the Igbo preserve some traditional practices that take care of the needs of the poor in their midst. In other words, the poor in traditional Igbo society do not lack in material need, not in absolute terms. On the one hand, this proverb stresses the necessity of *Aja*; in the Igbo traditional society, life depends on it. We recall that Basden (1966, p. 55) stated that sacrifice is an obligation that must be fulfilled by every adult. On the other hand, it is impossible for one not to have a thing to offer in sacrifice; thus, even the poor should have. Because life depends on it, *Aja* should be possible for all. Not to offer an oblation is to opt for death.

Okpori na-ekpori aja anaghi ekpori nke a chụrụ n'ajọ ọhịa. (Literarily: 'The scavenger that preys on *Aja* does not prey on the one offered in the evil forest.') The Igbo is aware that *Aja* is directly consumed by either human beings or animals. The *Aja* in question is the portion that is rightly due to the spirits. We have recognized the animal scavengers; now this proverb brings to mind that there are also human scavengers. *Ajọ-ọhia* is a thick bush reserved for the disposal of human beings who died due to certain illnesses understood as abominations. Metuh (1985) observed that

> immediately on the outskirts of the village is the ajo ohia, bad bush, where rubbish and all decaying matter is dumped. The bodies of the dead whose lives or deaths are utterly repugnant to the accepted religious standards are also unceremoniously dumped in the ajo ohia to symbolize total rejection and excommunication by both the living and the dead. (pp. 102-103)

Okpoli aja are those human beings who reserve the inalienable right over the materials used in sacrifice.

When I was young, growing up in my native town, Akpo in Aguata Local Government Area of Anambra State, little children from a neighbouring town, Amesi, would always confidently prey on consumable items used for sacrifice at various corners of my town. They would taunt us, "You people perform these sacrifices for us." Unlike them, we regarded those things used in sacrifices as sacrosanct and untouchable; we were taught never to meddle with them or open ourselves to the evil they were meant to avert. However, Amesi is noted for a wide variety of *Dibịaọgwụ*, and almost all the citizens are potential adepts in various types of *Ọgwụ* and *Anwansọ*. It must be noted that these days, no thanks to Christianity, those forms of sacrifices are rarely seen anymore, and the Amesi people are fast losing the secrets of Igbo science, which they had preserved.

Normal human beings do not enter *Ajọọhịa*; nobody, in fact, dares it except master adepts—*Dibịa*. This proverb tends to explain more about the terrific nature of *Ajọọhịa* than it informs about the impossibility of scavenging on *Aja* because those who can always do, no matter where. Nevertheless, we can decipher two important ideas about *Aja*. The first is that *Aja* that can even attract humans can be placed in *Ajọọhịa*. The second is that tangible and valuable things could be used as *Aja*, so that there can be human scavengers.

A chụọ aja ahụghị udene amara n'ihe mere na be ndị mmụọ. (Literarily: 'When sacrifices are offered and there are no vultures then all is not well in the abode of the spirits.') Vultures are scavengers. The portions of the animals used for sacrifice are dumped somewhere in the open air. Practically speaking, the sight of the vultures when the act of sacrifice is performed elates the heart of the Igbo and announces the arrival of the spirits. The vulture is a totem animal and is not killed throughout the Igbo country for any reason whatsoever. To kill it is a serious taboo, for vultures are seen as the souls or spirits who have come in the images of living things to take part in the sacrifice. It is not uncommon among the Igbo to understand animals and things as possessed by the spirits. If the Igbo abstain from killing an animal, the do so because such an animal may be the spirit of their ancestors. Many totem animals have such stories indicating they were emissaries from God, images of the progenitor of a race, saved a race or their progenitor from serious calamity, and so forth. In this proverb, the vultures are understood as representatives of the spiritual abode, whose presence affirms the efficacy of *Aja*.

There are other proverbs that have to do with *Aja* such as:

1. *A gana-achụ aja ka ikpe na-ama ndị mmụọ*: 'Sacrifices should be ceaselessly offered to make the spirit blameworthy for man's problems.'

2. *Aja ndụ bụ maka onye nọnụ na onye anọghọ*: 'A sacrifice for life is for everybody, present and absent.'

3. *Achụọ m aja dibịa ka m were jidere mmụọ ọfọ*: 'I have offered sacrifice as recommended by a priest so as to be upright before the spirits.'

4. *O na-abu akwara aja n'aka a na-ario ndi mmuo*: 'It is when one has one's sacrifice handy that one petitions the spirits.'

Chapter Twenty-two

Liturgies

Liturgies include the matters and forms of cultic rituals. *Matter* refers to the various materials used to perform a ritual while *form* refers to the words with which such rituals are accomplished. ITR is replete with endless elements having varied liturgies. We made a case in Chapter Eighteen that *Ichụaja* seems to be an indispensable part of various ITR rituals. Here, we intend to do a review of the *Irụagwọ* ritual to help us place *Ichụaja* in its rightful perspective. *The Agwụ* spirit is a sort of a spiritual manifestation of one's gift. The word *menace* is deliberately used because that is what the non-initiate understands, just like some non-initiates into the Christ mystery thought that the apostles were drunk or possessed on the morning of Pentecost. Umeh (1997, pp. 103ff) was elaborate in his treatment of the *Agwụ* spirit; with all respect, we indulge his excesses. E. Aguoji (Personal Communication, May 19, 2006) stated that, to perform the Irụagwụ ritual, these items are needed:

1. *Nnekwu Ọkụkọ* (Hen)
2. *Ụbụlụ* or *uriom Ọkụkọ* (Chicken)
3. *Egbene ọkụkọ* (Cock)
4. *Agidi Ọkụkọ* (Medium size chick)
5. *Akwa* (egg)
6. *Ọkụ* (earthenware basin)
7. *Nzu na Edo* (a kind of white and yellow chalk)
8. *Mbaji asatọ* (eight tubers of yam)
9. *Osisiakọnauche* (four short sticks from ogirisi or okwe tree)
10. *Ọjị* (Kola)

First, a spot is selected—a conspicuous part of the offerer's compound. A vegetative stem is planted on the spot, *Ogirisi*, for instance. Other items for the ritual—*nzu na edo, ụbụlụ ọkụkọ, ọjị,* and *akwa* are put inside the *ọkụ* and turned upside down beside the *ogirisi* stem, facing the east—*doo iru n'ọwụwa anyanwụ* ('source of the rising sun'). This part of the liturgy is called *Ikpu-ndi-akalogeli*. This rite signifies that the menacing spirit of *Agwụ*—*Akalogeli*—has been covered and chained in the *ọkụ*. This checks (symbolically) the possible abuse of the person's spiritual gift. Second, the *egbene* is used to touch the eyes and random parts of the body of the offerer. This action is accompanied by words that ask the menacing spirits to allow the offerer to employ his resources meaningfully. Afterwards the *egbene* is slain and its blood smeared on the four sticks. This rite is called *ihicha anya na iticha arụ*. Third, these sticks are tied with a string with accompanying words,— conjuring *mkpakọọnụ akọ na uche*discretionary use of the offerer's reasoning and intellect. This rite is called *ifie akọ na uche*. The tied sticks are handed over to the offerer who is asked to handle it with care and caution. He, most certainly, will be asked to do some sacrifices for the *akọ na uche* at regular intervals—*Ajaakọnauche*. Finally, the *nnekwu ọkụkọ* is killed and its blood poured on the spot, and the yams are ceremoniously presented to the new *Agwụ* deity. This last rite is called *Ịchụaja*.

A meal is prepared of the yams and *nnekwu ọkụkọ* while the *agidi ọkụkọ* is left to a free-range domestication as a property of the new *Agwụ* deity—*Ọkụkọ Agwụ*. It should be noted that the offerer does not participate in the meal, but every other person around is qualified to do so.

Ịchụaja is part of the ritual of *Ịrụagwọ*. *Agwụ*, it should be noted, is a spirit which besieges its victim, causing him to behave in an abnormal way. In his exposition, Umeh(1997) gave it the title of Holy Spirit. We must comment that the guru is not fully informed about the Holy Spirit. It is beyond the scope of this work to do a thorough pneumatological presentation, but suffice it to say that the Third Person of the Trinity—the Holy Spirit—cannot be reduced to *Agwụ*. Further, E. Aguoji (Personal Communication, May 19, 2006) disclosed that there are two modes in which *Agwụ* may manifest: *ezi agwụ* or *ajọ agwụ*. When one is possessed by *ezi agwụ*, he will compulsively be good to people, and whatsoever he does for people turns out to be a huge success, whereas things he does for himself hardly succeed. He is called to an altruistic ministry to votaries. One who is possessed by *ajọ agwụ* may experience what he called *akpa aghasa*. That is, whatever accrues from his endeavours will continue to fizzle away in mysterious ways. He can hardly retain meaningfully things he worked for, and whatever he engages in, ends in futility or disaster.

Scholars had understood *Ịchụaja* as an element in ITR that exhausts its own liturgy. In this work, we are coming to the conclusion that *Ịchụaja* is a moment in the liturgies of various elements in ITR characterized by the immolation of a victim. In all the elements we have discussed at various points in our exposition—*Ịtụegbo, Ịdọanyanwụnaezelu, Irunru, Ịrọmmụọ*, and so forth—we saw that *Ịchụaja* was always present in the liturgies. However, in the liturgies of *Ịchụogbunuke*, *Ịsaifi*, *Ịgbaaja*, or *Ịkpụarụ*, it does seem that *Ịchụaja* constitutes the only singular moment, and because there is normally no *oriri/orikọ* or communion in the liturgies of the whole elements constituting *Imedommụọ*, an external observer might think that they could altogether be referred to as *Ịchụaja*. Furthermore, *Ịkpụarụ* has two dimensions: for individual offence and community offence. Yet in either case, the mode of liturgy is the same. Sometimes the individual offence may not need the special assistance of the Nri High Priests for *Ịkpuarọ* ritual to be performed. Ogbukagu (1997) stipulates:

> There are two types of alu, namely *Aluluana* and *Alulugbada*. The *Alulugbada* is more serious than *Aluluana*. It (Alulugbada) constitutes the kind of alu that is exclusively cleansed by the Adama group themselves. The Aluluana can be cleansed by the Diodo Nri ... akin to alu, is Nso which is a mild type of Alu or abomination. (p. 45)

Furthermore, animals also break taboos in the traditional Igbo society. For instance, it is a taboo for a dog to give birth to just one puppy, a cow to give birth to more than one calf, a cock to crow at certain times of the day, a he-goat to mate a sheep, and so forth. Taboos such as these are often times categorized as *arụrụala* or *nsọ*. Some rituals are also performed on occasions like this for cleansing and may be done by any individual. Care must be taken that ideas in ITR are not confused. *Ịchụaja* is the figurative or symbolic but definitive ritual immolation of a victim offered to any of the objects of ITR—*Obinigwe/Ezelu/Osebulụwa* or *Ụmụmmụọ*; *Mmụọ dị icheiche*; *arụsọ*; or *ndiichie* (God or spirits, pure spirits, deities or ancestral spirits, disembodied spirits). This act is an indispensable part of every liturgy in the religion. In as much as Basden (1966, p. 157) has made us to understand *Ịchụaja* and *Ịchụogbunuke* to be one and the same thing, we understand with Metuh (1985) and Arinze (1970) if they misconstrue *Ịchụ* in both instances to imply one and the same thing. We now opine that *Aja* is 'victim' or 'oblation' while *ogbunuke* is 'menacing or malignant and capricious spirit.' *Ịchụogbunuke* is 'driving away the menacing or malignant and capricious spirits' while *Ịchụaja* is the ritual slaying of a victim or an oblation. But *driving away* is not the same as *annihilation* or *subjection*. Driving away is only from the local area of the offerer while the spirit in question goes on in its necessary role within the Igbo all-inclusive mystical ecosystem.

Chapter Twenty-three

Myths

Myths seem to have been relegated to the unscientific and primitive times in the history of human development. Nevertheless, they contain truths that can be psychological, religious, theological, and even philosophical. A myth points to a reality beyond itself, and Paul Ricouer referred to this as a "surplus meaning." In the opinion of Metuh (1981), "[Myth] … enhances the values as authentic vehicles of religious beliefs since such beliefs enjoy an appreciable degree of authenticity" (p. 29). ATR, like every other religion, makes abundant use of myths that contain accepted truths without any critical questions. More than the scientific basis or historicity of myths, their truths stand out clear to the mind of anyone who accepts them. Myths speak within the context in which they are used. It must be mentioned that the reluctance or inability of the mind to seek details in myths has caused and nurtured a lot of faith in so many believers who upheld mythical stories as historical and really true. Care must be taken in the study of myths to understand that the truth more than the fact is what matters. The religious truths represented in myths are more important than the factual nature of the information given in the mythical accounts. Most myths tell the origins and beginning of things, places, and peoples. According to Batto (1985): "Its story is 'timeless' and paradigmatic for the present; for this reason the story is often placed either in primordial time ('in the beginning') or in eschatological time after the present world has come to an end" (p. 698).

In one of the mythical accounts of the origins, which he referred to as Nri cosmology, Metuh (1985, pp. 38-39) stated that Eri is the progenitor of the Igbo race and his wife—*Namakụ*—had *Ọka* (the blacksmith) and *Diọka* (the cicatrisation expert) as company when God first sent him into the world. *Ọka* had the duty of drying the earth, which was in the form of a morass, with his bellows while *Diọka* did the *ichi* mark on the face of Eri (Ichi cicitrisation is to become one of the marks for which Eri's progenies will be known) and, especially his first son and daughter before the monumental sacrifice. Chukwu asked Eri to sacrifice his son and daughter. Eri did, but unlike Abraham of Jewish myth, God allowed Eri to kill his son and daughter. In their place, he gave Eri *ji* ('yam') and *ede* ('cocoyam'), which are the staple food of the Igbo culture. Thus, the son and daughter of Eri should properly be referred to as *Aja*.

In this myth, *Aja* represents a ransome paid to win divine favour. This myth is typical of ancient mythical accounts. It should be noted that—unlike the Babylonian Gilgamesh Epic or Atrahasis Story and unlike the Jewish Adam, Eve, and Noah—the Igbo myth of Eri lacked the causal line for God's demand of Eri's son and daughter. This missing link could be blamed on the fact that ITR has suffered an unchecked decline, especially in mystical advancement after its encounter with European civilization and Christianity. Otherwise, if one could do a redaction of the various mythical accounts of creation as was done of the four traditions in the Judeo-Christian Bible (Yahwist, Elohist, Deuteronomic, and Priestly), the Nri cosmology, Ibagwa cosmogony, Delta Group creation account, and Mbaise cosmogony could allow one to arrive at a single unbroken chain of the account of creation with negligible nuances; then, the question of the causal link as posed above would be answered. This redaction has already been attempted in chapter thirteen above; it could be furthered and fine-tuned. However, more than that, we are concerned with the role or function and the basic character of *Aja* as exposed in Igbo myths.

Between Eri and Chukwu, there must have been a severed concourse—the missing causal link. The demand made by Chukwu was to offer Eri a possibility of restoration. The divine-human link can only be restored through immolation and shedding of blood. Whatever Eri must have done to be shut off from the divine was paid for by the blood of his son and daughter. The Igbo had then to do like deeds again and again to open concourse with the divine severed by a profane human act. The Nri, who held this myth themselves, are descendants of priests who performed duties of reconciling erring humans with the divine. Being part of the myths of origins, the place of sacrifice in ITR could best be evaluated as central. It derives from the effort of man to restore a lost concourse with the divine. As long as the Igbo performed the ritual act of *Ichuaja*, he is rest assured that the world of the spirit is both open and favourable to him.

Another mythical account recorded by Umeh (1997, pp. 88-90) involving *Olisa-ekezu* and his rival friend—*Anyanwu-setoza* and her father, an ancient king—leaves much to be desired, though he excused his lack of details. Umeh (1997) posed the myth as "a most delightful and moving cosmogonic story of the origin of aja" (p. 88). It was *Olisa*—the Creator—who taught the benevolent Dibia and Olisa-ekezu how to perform sacrifice in order to confuse the *ndị mpụrụ chi ụwa* adverse forces and restore the lost testicles and penis of Olisa-ekezu. Umeh insinuated the idea of sacrifice, not just to God alone but to other malignant and capricious spirits as a means of confusing or manipulating them. This myth also consolidates the theory of Madu (2004), who averred that sacrifice is a magical means of manipulating the spirits. In all, *Ịchụaja* is a means of gaining favour from God and the spirits (Do ut Des).

Chapter Twenty-four

Folklore

Basden (1966) made an indelible remark about the Igbo in relation to folklore when he wrote: "He uses as illustrations animals and birds in such a way that they seem to be endowed with human powers. He can conjure up an atmosphere, and carry his audience with him, and thus provide thrilling entertainment" (p. 424). Beyond arts and entertainment, the Igbo also aim at ethical reflections and proffering truths about ultimate reality, especially the "how"of things, even in folklore. The teller employs mimicry, facial expressions, and gesticulations to make the stories come alive. Sometimes, the details of such stories are used most uncritically.

A classical folklore about *Aja* goes thus: Once upon a time, a dispute arose among the animals about which of them should be used by humans for the purpose of sacrifice. The controversy was such that none of them agreed to be used as a victim, not even the lion in all its ferocity. At last, they all agreed to make a journey to Chukwu's abode for him to give the final verdict on the issue. The domestic fowl was a jolly good fellow who would not delight in taking all the stress of the journey to Chukwu's abode. When pressed too hard to join the league with an ultimatum, the unsuspecting fowl said to the other animals, "Go ye to the deliberation and bring back news to me. Whatever you all agree upon and is endorsed by Chukwu, I'll definitely accept in good faith." So the animals went forth. On their way, the tortoise interrupted the journey and suggested that it would be better if they did this deliberation once more and take their decision to Chukwu. Agreeing, the animals inquired once again who would come forward to this victimhood. When no one braved it, the tortoise then spoke up, "The domestic fowl told us that he will in good faith accept whatever be our deliberation on this matter, provided it is endorsed by Chukwu. Therefore, it would be tantamount to no injustice if we were to decide that he (the domestic fowl) becomes the veritable victim of all human sacrifices." Finding the suggestion of the tortoise plausible, the animals unanimously agreed to take the same verdict to Chukwu. Consequently, Chukwu ratified the decision that the domestic fowl would be the commonest victim of human sacrifices. All the animals happily went home, carrying the news to the domestic fowl, who lamented his fate to no avail. Up until the present day, the domestic fowl is the commonest victim of sacrifice done by humans. There is scarcely a sacrifice in ITR without the domestic fowl one way or another.

This story is also meant to teach the moral lesson that one ought to make one's self available when issues of community interest are to be deliberated upon in order to contribute one's own bit. It shows the democratic nature of the Igbo world, yet the idea of a victim for sacrifice being an animal is not silent. The story highlights the following:

1. The necessity of blood in any sacrifice.

2. The central place of the domestic fowl in all sacrificial acts.

When this story is told in its proper manner and language, the word used to describe the act of sacrifice is *Ịchụaja*. The slaying of *Aja* is a religious exercise, though it must be noted that scarcely any slaying in Igbo culture is profane. Even when the purpose is to produce meat, there is a religious undertone to it.

PART SEVEN

FUNCTIONS OF ỊCHỤAJA
IN IGBO RELIGIOUS CULTURE

Chapter Twenty-five

Religious Function

It has already been seen that *Ichuaja* sustains the Igbo, assuring him of a continual interaction with the spiritual world. *Ichuaja* is a ritual both practical and ideological, with which the Igbo penetrate the closed area of the spirit. Votaries of ITR operate at two levels:

1. *Omara* (the Knowers): To this group belongs the *dibia*. The *dibia* is an initiate into the mysteries and mystical knowledge of ITR. The possession of knowledge gives him an edge over all other votaries of the religion. We use the word *dibia*, cognizant of the fact of the various categories there are which at the same time, are not in our interest to discuss. So, whether it is *Dibiaafa*, *Dibiaaja*, *Dibiaogwu*, or Arazu's (2003, p. 11) *Dibiaojenammuo*, each in his own right belongs to the class of *Omara*. Umeh (1997, p. 76) captured the English translation of *dibia* in the words *master*, *adept*, or *expert in knowledge and wisdom*. All other votaries may be experts or adepts in one or more fields in the Igbo world, like the *Dimgba* or *Diji*

159

and so forth, but the *Dibịa*, like the Aristotelian "man of theoria," is a free spirit trained in the knowledge of *ousia*, *substantia*, *essentia*, and *energeia* while the former are like men of practical knowledge or artisans. It must be noted that these adepts hold the knowledge of whatever aspect wherein they specialize in secrecy.

2. *Ofeke* (the non-knowers): Every other votary may belong to this group. Without philosophy, this group understands the practical nature of ITR and practices it as such. They are ignorant in terms of not knowing even the essential things about God, being, and things.

We did this division based on the saying, "*A tụọrọ ọmara ọmara, a tụọrọ ofeke ofenye ịsị n'ọhịa.*" (The adept always deciphers the hidden truth in the code while the non-knower is lost in the sea of possibilities.) However, there is a possible third group that we cannot easily categorize among these two: *Nwadibia* or *dibịanchụaja*. This class is principally charged with the duty of performing the practical sacrifice for the people. He is not a priest of any particular deity, but either works in the employ of any class of *dibịa* as mentioned above or in partnership with them, though as a kind of junior colleague. This class does not know as much as does the *Ọmara*, but knows better than the *Ofeke* and sometimes appears as an apprentice to the *dibịa*. In fact, Umeh (1997) described this class thus: "Nwadibia is essentially an ofeke (non-dibia) who through very laborious and time consuming long studies and the ritual process of *isa/isanye/isata ọgwụ* learns herbs and some *Ọgwụ* from the *dibịa* and sets out to practice those he so acquired" (p. 80). *Nwadibịa* is not knowledgeable in spiritual dynamics but specializes in practical ritualizations recommended to him. Notice that the *Dibịaafa* does the divining and speaks the mind of the spirits and *Nwadibịa* does the practical rituals while the *Dibịaaja* stands in lieu of a particular deity to which sacrifice is made, speaking and acting in *persona deitatis*. *Dibịaaja* is properly designated in ITR as *Ezemmụọ* or *Ezearụsị*.

It was Immanuel Kant who differentiated between practical and pure reason after the assertion of Aristotle in his stratification of society. In the same Kantian manner``````, we assert that *Dibịa* is a man of pure (spiritual) reason while *Nwadibịa* is a man of practical reason. Umeh (1997) was elaborate in the treatment of these issues, but it may be necessary for us to say here that *Afa* is the highest mode of Igbo epistemology while *Ojenammụọ* is the highest form of metaphysics, and it is the *dibịa* who attends either or both feats. As in the Hindu religion, one's attitude towards *Aja* could help to discern the level of one in religious awareness—*Ọmara* or *Ofeke*—in ITR. For instance, the *Ọmara* understands the ritual import of *Ụkpaaja*; the mystical connotation of *Uriom Ọkụkọ*; the spiritual implication of *Nkịrịnka Akwa*, *Mkpụrụ ji*, and *Mkpụrụ ego*; the numerological value of *Ezi gbara ịtọ*; and the extent of cosmic energy generated in a singular stride of *Ịchụaja* involving all of these. He knows the dynamics involved in energizing the spiritual terrain with simple matter. The *Ofeke*, on the other hand, is not just ignorant of all these but bothers nothing about them. His involvement is simply practical to the extent that he thinks much to much about the matter that he confronts. If we may employ Vedic categorizations in this instance, the *Ọmara* sacrifices in the mode of goodness or knowledge, like Brahmas; the *Nwadibịa* sacrifices in the mode of passion, like Ksatriyas; the *Ofeke* sacrifices in the mode of ignorance, like Sudras.

In the definition of *sacrifice* given by Ekwunife (n.d., *Lecture Note*, p.62) quoted earlier in this work, he insinuated that sacrifice is a prayer. It is the idea of *Do ut des* that dominates the motivation of the Igbo in performing *Ịchụaja*. The Igbo is aware of the spirits that share concourse with them in the same environment and strives to live in concord and harmony with them. *Ịchụaja* affords him the medium in which to achieve this. The social interaction among the Igbo does not involve only humans; it includes spirits. For such a society to thrive, there must be a forum for the interaction of entities that do not belong to the same mode of existence. For the Igbo this forum is *Ichuaja*. It is a moment, mode and means of bringing the separated worlds together precisely for the good of man. It is one single act that is performed or could be performed by the votary of ITR.

Chapter Twenty-six

Social Function

As the Igbo seek harmony with the spirits, so do they seek harmony with their fellow men. The saying *"egbe bere ugo bere nke si ibe ya ebena nku kwapụ ya"* ('let the kite perch and the eagle besides, whichever undermines the perching of another, may it have its wing broken') is an essential part of every Igbo prayer, a kind of "live and let live." This cosmic harmony, based on the natural laws of "action and reaction are equal and opposite" and *"ọbịara be onye abịagbuna ya, mgbe ọ ga-ana mkpukpu apụna ya"* ('let the guest not inflict harm on his host so that on his way home, he may not be inflicted with a hunch-back'), has been altered by some Christian phantasmic ideas to no avail. Now, the saying has other nuances like *egbe bere ugo bere nke si ibe ya ebena o gosi ya ebe ọ ga-ebe* ('let the kite perch and the eagle besides, whichever undermines the perching of another should show it where to perch') modulated by Christians to portray love of enemy.

However, in whatever manner it is presented, it brings forth the harmonious coexistence of people perennially sought by the Igbo.

Ịchụaja guarantees this harmony. When people take part together in an act of sacrifice, they profess this harmonious co-existence. In the Igbo culture, enemies cannot take part together in an act of sacrifice because, as enemies, they cannot partake together in the spiritual communion—*Orikọ*—that is an essential part of every sacrifice in the category of *Ajanchụnye*. Participating together in a sacrificial meal underscores a tie between participants and the spirits. Okpalansofor (Personal Communication, April 23, 2006) said to me, "*Aja di ire bu obi gbara na nnaa.*" ('An efficacious sacrifice is one offered with the unity of hearts.') At every act of sacrifice, the Igbo avail themselves of a fresh opportunity to enter into a new covenant or renew an existing one. A covenant serves as one means through which the Igbo are assured of peace and tranquility in a world full of strife and unprecedented threats. Even in their new religious experiences, the Igbo have not outgrown this idea.

It is curious when Igbo Christians request *Ịgbandọ* from time to time, especially the Roman Catholics whose covenant theology is unrivalled in the whole of Christendom. In the Catholic Church, every Eucharistic celebration is a sacrifice aimed at the renewal of the covenant in Christ. If the Igbo understand and accept the efficaciousness of this sacrifice, then they should employ the same attitude that has been an essential part of the Igbo life. In this sense, *Ịchụaja* serves the Igbo as a means of unification for all. When things are not all well with everybody together, it is by means of *Ịchụaja* that all dissenting parties are brought together in a communion of unity, mostly in the form of covenant. However, within this frame of thought, *Ịchụaja* and *Ịgbandụ* should not be understood to mean one and the same thing. We rather insinuate that *Ịchụaja* is interiorly oriented towards effecting a mystical bonding of the lives of participants. As Njoku (2002) rightly observes, "The transition from inter-personal and family conflicts to community or social conviviality was mostly wrought by covenant establishing peace among persons and groups" (p. 184). *Ịchụaja* is also an essential part of the rites of covenant: *Igbandụ*.

Chapter Twenty-seven

Political Function

We subscribe to the opinion that the Igbo political system is democratic in the line of thought of Ejiofor (1981). Ejiofor was more interested in behavioural analysis and he had no space for other aspects of Igbo democratic disposition. Beyond this analysis, we assert that it is *Afa* that has a prominent role to play in Igbo traditional politics because democratic consensus in the Igbo world involves the living and the dead in traditional society. As it were, the opinion of the dead is sought over and above that of the living; the dead have a pride of place, for they have successfully traversed the various regions of existence and can be referred to as triumphant. The knowledge of the *Dibịaafa* transcends the human terrains; therefore, he is capable of seeking and finding the opinion of the spirits in human affairs, even in politics. However, the knower in ITR can employ *Ịchụaja* to penetrate the spiritual terrain and influence the opinion of the spirits, either by direct demand by the spirits or by an extraordinary knowledge of the mind of the spirits. Perhaps, this is what Madu (2004) meant by *manipulation*.

Ịgbanjaahọ or *Igbandụ* is an element in ITR that appears silent in all our discourse. This element has been mentioned in passing while dealing with the social function of *Ịchụaja*. However, tt is pertinent to note that every occasion of *Ịchụaja* smacks of *Ịgbandọ*. By paying homage to the spirit, man ritually covenants himself to that spirit. One might call this the implicit consequence of *Ịchụaja*. There is always a covenant or contract between the votary and an object of religion in any instance of spiritual or sacramental contact. However, in the Igbo world, *Ịgbanjaahụ* or *Ịgbandụ* is a practice often undertaken to strike the essential harmonic chord among the people. It is a means of assuring everyone that everyone is everyone's keeper. In it, the spirits are invited to be present at the ritual communion of man. Even today in the new religious experience of the Igbo, the practice still exists. Political consensus is often sealed in *Ịgbandọ*, which also has *Ịchụaja* as part of its liturgy. Okpalansofor (Personal Communication, April 23, 2006) underscored the relationship between *Ịgbanjaahọ* and *Ịchụaja* when he said, "*Ọọ aja k'adị chụọrọ ndị ochie mbụ, ndị mmadụ were rikọọ, ňụkọọ, ňụrịa. Ọọ ya bụ Ịgbanjaahụ. Ma e je-eme ya n'okwu mmụọ.*" ('It is a ransom which is paid to the ancestors while men eat, drink and make merry together. That is the idea of covenant which must be done before a deity.') The recent story of the Okija shrine in Anambra State of Nigeria where politicians went for the *Ịgbandọ* ritual to consolidate trust among themselves is a case study of the survival of such practices. It is the blood of the covenanting parties that is important in the *Ịgbandụ* ritual. *Ịchụaja* has a political relevance both in attending the dead and consolidating trust among the living to come to a consensus in Igbo democracy. Consensus in Igbo democracy is understood as a bond that has a serious religious implication.

Chapter Twenty-eight

Economic Function

The Igbo's is basically a sedentary culture. Evidence of migration within the culture area did not affect the basic idea of life for the people. Farming, especially of the root-crop 'ji', formed the principal source of their economy. Economic power was measured by *Ọba Ji*, that is, the strength of one's yam-barn. At the beginning of every planting season, the man is expected to perform a ritual before the family shrine. In Akpo Aguata Local Government Area, Anambra State, the man comes in front of the shrine with his farm implements and presents them to the family deity. He then brings objects, four in number (palm kernnels or something else), representing the four days of the week—*Afọ*, *Nkwọ*, *Eke* and *Orie*—and places them in front of the deity. He covers them with *ọkụ* (an earthenware basin). This is called *Ikpuọbụbọ*. He prays that no *Ọbụbọ* will catch up with him throughout the planting season. (*Ọbụbọ* is a kind of omen, which might cause him to wound himself with the farm implement). He offers sacrifice in accordance with his economic power, perhaps a chicken. This is called *Ịchụaja*. He then asks the spiritual assistance of the deity and the ancestors for a problem-free planting.

Metuh (1985, p. 135) describes a community ritual before the planting season in which *Ịchụaja* and *Orikọ* are major features, and Ekwunife (1990, p. 93) made a diagrammatic representation of consecratory rites in the agricultural calendar of Aguleri. These rites depict the significance of religious activity in the economic arena. Ritual activities, of which *Ịchụaja* is a principal part, have an agricultural calendar, and it was agriculture that was the main economic strength of the Igbo. Even today when the Igbo, like the Jew, retain trading as their main economic activity, they still look for spiritual assistance through *Ịchụaja*. When they offer sacrifices in their new religious professions, it is with the hope that God will grant increase to their businesses (*Do ut des*). More than a radical economic power informed by thoroughgoing capitalism, the Igbo seeks egalitarian well-being informed by community spirit. It is the spirits who are the dispensers of this well-being. The proverbs go a long way to show that the spirits should confirm the efforts of man before well-being is achieved: *Okụbalụ ma chi ekweghi onye ụta atala ya.* ('Whoever makes a sincere human effort but has nothing to show for it because his *chi* has not confirmed his efforts should not be blamed for his woes.') *Onye chi ya na-etiri akị amaghị ihe ndị na-ebu nkume na-ahụ.* ('Those whose *chi* crack their palm kernnels may not be bothered about what those who carry stones suffer.') *Chi nwa ogbenye anaghi efo ọsọọsọ.* ('The poor man's day takes time to dawn.') *Ejighị oke igba ụzọ agbapụ chi ọjọọ.* ('Early starters may not by such means evade misfortunes.') *Onye chi ọjọọ kpatara nkụ, ewu taa ya.* ('It is the unfortunate man who gathered dry wood and they were consumed by the goat.') Consequently, the Igbo meet his part of the bargain with the spirit by *Ịchụaja*.

Chapter Twenty-nine

Psychological Function

The *dibịa* in ITR is also a great psychologist. He employs a good deal of intuition, which has been trained over time. The Igbo say, "*Ịdụ n'ubu ka dibịa ji agbara ofeke afa.*" ('With a mere shoving of the shoulders, the *dibịa* does divination for the *ofeke.*') The gnoseological gap between the *Ọmara* and the *Ofeke* gives the former an edge to employ mere psychological manipulation on the later. In many cases, *Ịchụaja* may not necessarily be effective, based on its potentials to open up the area of the spirits, but on the psychological effect it has on the *Ofeke* who offers it. On a second level, the Igbo think that once *Ịchụaja* has been accomplished, every human possibility has been exhausted. The following sayings portray the psychological state of the Igbo after he has done his utmost—*Ịchụaja*: *A gana-achụ aja ka ikpe na-ama ndị mmụọ.* ('Sacrifices should constantly be offered so that whatever is lacking in the well-being of man may be blamable on the spirits.') *Achụọ m aja dibịa ka m jidere mmụọ ọfọ.* ('I have performed the sacrifice as recommended by the diviner that I may be righteous before the spirits.') *Ịchụaja* gives the Igbo a psychological disposition to go on with a life which may otherwise be very frustrating. Most often, the *Ofeke* understands religious practices as magic. Practical experience has shown too that ignorance fans the embers of faith, especially in the magical. Interestingly, somehow this magic from time to time works. It is the psychological disposition of the votary that blinds him to possibilities in nature and affords him undivided focus on the religious and spiritual. *Ịchụaja* is one of those religious activities that fill the votary, especially the ignorant non-initiate, with psychological energy.

PART EIGHT

EVALUATION, SUMMARY, AND CONCLUSION

Evaluation

The Igbo universe is a complex whole; it is one but dualized. It is not *Eluigwe* ('Heaven') *na* ('and') *Ụwa* ('Earth') as has been introduced by Christian thought but *Igwe* ('the sky') *na* ('and') *Ala* ('the earth'); nor is it *Eluigwe* ('Heaven') *na* ('and') *Ọkummụọ* ('Hell') of Christianity but *Bemmụọ* ('spirit's abode') *na* ('and') *Bemmadụ* ('man's abode'). This duality is true only at the level of phenomenological interpretation of reality, beyond which unity in the One takes over. The mystical One is the area of harmony of all things, where nothing is left out, nothing neglected. *Igwe na Ala* divided by a vertical distance are more abodes of deities than abodes of different kinds of being. These deities are phenomenological figures representing the mystical distance between men and spirits. *Bemmụọ na Bemmadọ* are abodes of different kinds of beings that are co-existent in this terrestrial region. The spirits are always present within the domains of humans in spite of their mystical apartness.

In ITR, it is the harmony of this complex world and existence that is sought in the practical area of *Ịchụaja*.

This work has not proved to be an easy one for a couple of reasons. At first, it appeared as though the writer did not appreciate the work done by earlier scholars in ITR, especially in the area of *Ịchụaja*. However, it can only be said that they set a worthy precedent. Beyond that, examining ITR, as it is, has become necessary and there remains much work to be done, especially now that we are becoming more aware and independent in thought. The present writer neither has sympathy for any religion to which he may be affiliated, nor is he opposed to the ideas of such a religion. What *I believe* does not make nonsense of what *I don't believe*. It is all a matter of faith, which subjected to thorough reasoning is always foolish, in any case. For this same reason, the method of Ekwunife (1990), participant observation, was employed.

Participation in this work included indulging in the thoughts of the religion even when they could be judged outrageous by the already widely accepted criteria. At the same time, ITR may not be taken in total isolation as though it lacked the basic principles and motivations of religion even in its antiquated garb. A religion must have a consistent system and subsistent object to be worthy of the name. It is unfair to dismiss the whole of ITR as mere primitivity simply because some other religious systems and ideas have been accepted (by dint of conspiracy) as world religions. This book was a sincere and sustained effort to come to ITR with basic religious principles and find its object, system, and idea on those principles. For instance, we were able to say that the fundamental object of ITR is *Mmụọ*: *Obinigwe (Ezechitoke Abiama), Umu mmụọ* (good and evil alike), *Arụsọ*, and *Ndiichie*. The appellation *Mmụọ* expands the nature of the God of ITR.

The object of ITR worship is both One and Many. As One, it encompasses Many in one Supreme Being; as Many, it is a hierarchy of existence under one Supreme Head.

This work also sought the basic idea of *Ịchụaja*, not just in the ability of votaries and scholars to interpret it, but with the somewhat silent tool of "what religious sense it makes." *Ịchụaja* as "driving away evil" makes no religious sense at all in as much as it is the heart of ITR. This truth is more appreciated when the liturgies of the various elements found in the religion are examined and their various moments properly categorized. It was found that there is always a moment referred to as *Ịchụaja*. The translation of "driving away evil" was born by the isolation of *Ịchụaja* as an element distinct from others. A possible reason for such isolation was also suggested.

Nevertheless, we acknowledge the seeming confusion that arose when the words *Ajanchụpụ* and *Ajanchụnye* were employed. In the first place, they were coined by the writer for two reasons. One was that one of those interviewed, Mr. Marcel Ugwu of Obukpa in Nsukka, observed: "*Ịchụpụ aja na Ịchụnye aja abụghi ofu ihe.*" (*To sacrifice away* and *to sacrifice to* are not the same thing.) Pardon my poor translation, I cannot do better. The Igbo version was very clear. He simply said this in the course of discussion, and then it brought up the idea of the objects of ITR, which included what Christian thought has caused us to understand as evil spirits. The Igbo knew "menacing spirits," but they did not judge them as fundamentally evil. Their menacing activities were justified, so they qualify for some sacrifice. We remember the words of M. Okpalaonyido (Personal Communication, April 24, 2006) of Akpo in Aguata Local Government Area of Anambra State: "*Chukwu kere ekwensu kee agwụ, hapụ onye ọbụna ka ọ kpara ọnụ ya.*" (It is God who created these menacing spirits; it is important to know that he left them free to fend for themselves.)

Even God Himself is not entirely immune to this possibility of menacing votaries. In the Jewish kabala, the element of the *sefirot—Keter*—is both crown and nothingness. The tension generated by the dialectics of these two poles is represented in human language as emotive. Thus, God could be said to be angry or jealous, qualities which are regarded as imperfections. It is the mystical understanding of what might be called the "evil" side of God that made Job reply to his wife in the manner he did when she taunted him, "Why do you still hold fast to your integrity? Curse God and die" (Job 2:9). Job replied: "You talk as any impious woman might talk. If we accept good from God, *shall we not accept evil?*" (Job 2:10). The Revised Standard Version used the phrase "foolish women," which is closer to the Igbo *Ofeke*. Job's wife is certainly a non-initiate of the kabala, so she does not have a profound understanding of the dynamism in God; Job—*Ọmara*—knew and was strong in it.

This idea is sustained even in Christianity for which suffering, mortification, and even death could be seen in a positive light, and the suffering and death of Christ Himself possibly justified. Likewise in ITR, *Agwụ, Ekwensu, Akalogeli, Ogbunuke*, and so forth are menacing spirits and at the same time agents of the ultimate goal of the religion: cosmic equilibrium or harmonious concourse of the universe and man, spirits and man, and man with his fellow men. That is the idea of *"egbe bere ugo bere nke sị ibe ya ebena, nku kwaa ya."* (Live and let live, contrary to which there is consequence.) This consequence beyond retribution makes for equilibrium. Consequent upon this, sacrifices to menacing spirits are very common. At the same time, no spirit is interiorly oriented to menace; spirits are spirits and can be at one time or another benevolent or malevolent.

The second reason for the coinage was that the word *Ịchụaja* in contemporary Igbo translates 'sacrifice,' no thanks to Christianity. Here and throughout the work, it was a difficulty to dispense with this concept. The writer battled with this frustrating bias. In spite of that, the categories of *Ajanchuụpụ* and *Ajanchụnye* were based on mode, which was deemed the best form of categorization in the sacrificial systems by the writer. In either case, it is important to note that the categories, new as they might sound, have been developed for the purpose in this study of relieving the word *Ịchụaja* of the burden of the Western-Christian idea of sacrifice.

Summary and Conclusions

From the beginning of the work, we stated clearly that we are agitated by the position of scholars about sacrifice in ITR. This position clearly understood *Aja* as 'evil' and *Ịchụaja* as 'driving away evil.' We made an initial evaluation that it made no religious sense if pursuing evil is the principle guiding the idea of sacrifice and that the idea itself contradicts or made nonsense of the Igbo world view upon which is built its religious ideas. Even though until now ITR has been one of those religions relegated to the class of primitive, pagan, and fetish expressions and, worse still, has suffered neglect as a result of the arrogation of world religions (e.g., Christianity, Islam, and Hinduism) to some selected expressions, ITR should, nevertheless, have basic elements of religion to make it worthy to be called a religion. We consider the position of former scholars as evidently biased by this arrogance.

In this work, we exercised a good bit of sympathy for ITR and, without bias, represented the ideas of the religion in a more positive light with the method of participant observation. We were also motivated by the thought that it could be possible to categorize ITR as a world religion depending on the criteria of this categorization. Various tools were used in accomplishing this arduous task. Prominent is the phenomenological and hermeneutical analysis of the world view, language, culture, and philosophy of the Igbo. Our diversified exercise in phonology, morphology, syntax, and semantics informed us that *Ịchụ* relates more to 'slay' than to 'drive away.' The climax of this work was the taxonomical analysis of the semantic representations of some concepts related to *Ịchụaja* in Igbo cultic ritual elements. It is important to note that what an average mind will understand as a negative force or agent opposed to the proper object of any religion is understood to be the other side of the same coin and this thought is not peculiar to ITR. Unlike contemporary Christian interpretations, sacrifices are rendered even to such spirits, forces, or agents without contradiction to the proper object of the religion. This fact forms the mainstay of misconstrual of *Ịchụaja* as meaning 'driving away evil.' On the one hand, there is the lack of the knowledge about the deep things of the spirit while, on the other hand, there is the acceptance of the Christian idea of good and evil, both militating against the objective judgement of the scholar. Even at that, *Aja* cannot be 'Menace' (which is more acceptable to us), nor can *Ịchụ*, in this rendition, imply 'pursue' or 'drive away.'

It became necessary to extend the search to oral tradition, in which we considered names, proverbs, liturgies, myths, and folklore. We then established that the form of sacrifice referred to by Basden (1966), Arinze (1970), Metuh (1985), and Umeh (1997) as paid to malicious and capricious spirits could also be rendered to any object of ITR—*Obinigwe* (*Ezechitokeabiama*), *ụmụmmmụọ*, *arụsị*, or *ndiichie*—precisely because any of them can constitute a menace to humans. Also, the victim proper for this exercise is not despicable as Arinze (1970) thought, in the sense of insignificant but could be anything at all that is prescribed by *Afa*. It is *Afa* that gives the specifications for *Aja*.

In concluding this work, we affirm that *Ichuaja* is the heart of practical Igbo traditional religion. In as much as this statement is true, its being understood will not be taken for granted. Being the heart of ITR is understood to mean that the exercise is performed as though there were no more to the religion but just that and that everything depends on it. Its variances and variability cannot be exhausted because *Afa* can come up with what has not been done or known before. Practically speaking, it is also understood as mystical. However, the exercise is not empty of all logic, philosophy, and reason. Therefore, it was necessary for us to state the various classes in ITR with which we could assert the rationale behind the sacrosanctity and exclusivity of knowledge beyond the practical. *Omara*, the class of *dibia*, have the secret knowledge of the rationale behind the practical and are vowed to sacrosanctity and secrecy. They know and can see that there is more than the external performance of *Ichuaja*. Being the highest form of knowledge, *Afa* recommends exercises as they are properly and mystically related to the occasions for which they are performed.This work has proved ITR to be a practical religion; the kind in which the world view that host it could pose a comprehensive and comprehensible philososphy. It is the ability of the votary to observe all the varied and variegated practices especially those recommended by *Afa* which marks him or her as an ardent practitioner. Meanwhile, there is no singular practice that does not require *Ichuaja*. Therefore at the heart of this practical religion is *Ichuaja* as one consistent, constant and continuing event. At this point, we define that *Ichuaja* is the practical immolation of a victim recommended by *Afa* as apt to the situation with which *Afa* is confronted and is believed by the Igbo to be the singular means of righting the wrong of humans in the judgement of *Mmụọ*—be it wrong moral, social, political, economic, or otherwise—by paying due homage or regular commemoration of whatever *Mmụọ* and entreating, invoking, or conjuring *Mmụọ* for a favour.

The word *Ịchụaja* is composed of two words: *Ịchụ* and *Aja*. This research concludes that, while *Ịchụ* is 'slay,' *Aja* is 'victim.' *Ịchụaja* is, in a concise manner, 'the slaying of the victim': *sacer ficere*. Therefore, the word *Ịchụaja*, being the heart of ITR, could translate the Christian idea of sacrifice, which also is the central event in the life of Christ—the central object of Christianity. The Catholic understanding of the sacrifice of Christ is both *Ajanchụnye*—the Last Supper—and *Ajanchụpọ*—death (perfect obedience and immolation) at Calvary. Properly speaking, *Ịchụaja* has the character of immolation and oblation among all other elements of the sacrificial system in ITR. Furthermore, whether it is *Ịchụaja* or *Aja*, both can be used to translate *sacrifice* because *Ịchụ* could, in very many circumstances, be elided to reduce possible cumbersomeness in expression. Therefore, wherever *Aja* is used to translate *sacrifice*, the idea of Ịchụ is present but silent. However, it may be more convenient to say that while *Aja* is the noun form meaning 'sacrifice,' *Ịchụaja* is its verb form, expressing the action performed in sacrifice, which we say is immolation. Once the victim is slain, the Igbo have ritually accomplished the goal of his religious quest. It is the theory of *do ut des* that succinctly captures the idea of *Ịchụaja* in ITR. Finally, whether it is in the Vedic religions, Judaism, or Christianity, immolation seems to be a consistent quality of sacrifice, even in the form of fasting. It is only in this kind of understanding that the practice of ITR in *Ịchụaja* could make some religious sense. *Aja* is both 'victim' and the noun form of 'sacrifice' while *Įchųaja* is the verb form of 'sacrifice.' In both instances, they can be understood as generic.

Recommendations

In all facets of human life, the West has arrogated to itself a paradigmatic status. The tools available to scholars in various dimensions of human endeavour, especially in Africa, have been offered by the West. The authenticity, veracity, scientific nature, and effectiveness of anything depend on how far it is in agreement or disagreement with the ever available Western paradigm. We advocate that Africans, as far as they can afford to, must divest themselves of the Western tools in their possession whenever they are undertaking the study of anything African. If it is a Herculean task to present such things in a positive light, it should, at least, be possible to present them as they are in agreement with common human sense. The time has come for us to tell our stories ourselves in the languages and categories that we are at home with, not borrowing the evaluation of another about us (except when such a one could be correct), not allowing others to tell our story in language and categories both foreign to us and poor in themselves for conveying the enormous richness of our lot.

Religion is a very complex area, filled with personal, interior, and esoteric experiences that are part of its truth. Care must be taken that personal interpretations do not shadow the objective truths in the study of any religious element. The method of participant observation has proved to be very helpful in ameliorating this hazard. ITR seem to be among the worst hit by Western ideological and intellectual invasion of Africa. It has suffered the double-barreled attack of misrepresentation on the part of Western anthropologists, who had an overwhelming influence on our early elites, and a programmed extinction on the part of the Igbo themselves, who are blindly held in the sway of this program, schemed by the same West.

However, before us is a possible collapse of the ungrounded alternative we inherited form the West—new religious affiliations in the name of Christianity—because we either do not understand the idea they are built on or have failed to build our own foundation (on our traditional world view) to ground its truth. It should be more than urgent for Africans, especially Igbo, to undertake studies like this themselves and in sympathy with the object of their study. Consequent upon this undertaking, there are five elements in ITR that need to be given serious and well-researched attention if this inherited Christianity will survive the current fundamentalist arsenal. They are *Ịchụaja, Ịgbaafa, Ibuarụsị, Ịdaọgwụ*, and *Imedibịa*. Efforts should be made to study them in such a way that the belief systems in ITR may be systematically presented with a consistent guiding logic. Arm-chair speculations and Husserlian method of "the epoche of being" will no longer be acceptable, especially in Africa where reality is all-inclusive. Phenomenology in African studies should, therefore, seek both correspondence and coherence of one reality to another in one stride of bracketing reality. This task of fairness to ITR in our study of its elements is not for the glory of ITR but for a more profound appreciation of the new religious experiences of our movement.

Limitations of the Work

A work like this one cannot claim to be exhaustive because of the constraints of both time and space. This work did not go into the details of examining objects prescribed for sacrifices so as to expose their cultic significance and possibly arrive at a comprehensive sacrificial law as seen of Judaism in the book of *Leviticus*. Given time and space too, this feat may not be easy to achieve because no one preempts *Afa*, and *Afa* does not thrive in uniformity. Evidently, cultic ritual activities in ITR are neither formalized nor uniformized. Nevertheless, the kind of ritual activity required in certain circumstances may be known outside *Afa*; what *Afa* does is to stipulate other details that might come up as different in a similar case elsewhere. It all depends on *Afa*. For instance, the Jew can say, if a priest is guilty of any public sin of adultery, a bull is needed for his cleansing because it is the inner sanctuary that is thus desecrated. On the contrary, the Igbo cannot say this because *Afa* may request that a sacrifice of a cow be done in one case and recommend a goat in another.

Ultimately, this work questioned the religious idea behind the core practical element of ITR, so it is not merely a phenomenological exposition of the practice. Therefore, prescriptive code cannot be found in this work. In as much as the work identified *Įchŷaja* as a moment in various liturgies, it did not bother to elaborate further on that particular moment, exploring its mystical significance. Nevertheless, it is a fair attempt to begin research into the anthologies of *Afa* as regards *Įchŷaja*, having conquered the ground of its predominant idea.

Suggestions for Further Research

It is possible to outline a prescriptive sacrificial law through the study of the various occasions of *Įchŷaja* and comparison of the cases. Scholars of ITR should aim at systematizing the religion in such a way that it could have a studied consistency for easier research and practice by those interested. The idea is simply to conform with the Western scientific methodology and formalization of studies. Modern researchers may not be comfortable with Igbo

(African) method, which requires the rigours of initiation and oath of secrecy with stringent measures attached.

Contributions of This Research

This research has examined the sacrificial system in ITR while being mindful of its counterparts in other religions. It has offered a new etymological appreciation of the word *Ịchụaja* and made its concept more acceptable and congruous with sacrificial ideas of other religions. *Ịchụaja* is not just a mere pagan and fetish practice; it has deep religious meaning, which this research has tried to bring to light. We believe that the whole idea of sacrifice in ITR has been radicalized and made more profound and meaningful. Before this work, *Ịchụaja* has been viewed from a negative perspective; this work has opened further vistas to the understanding of what the votaries of ITR do in a more positive light. In the coinages offered, the work contributed words that could be used to distinguish one form of sacrifice from another based on mode. The classification of cultic rituals here is the first of its kind and is open to positive modifications, provided that its aim of making the religion more comprehensive and practicable is achieved. The work also has presented the object of ITR in one word, which simultaneously accommodates the various nuances in the religion, thereby making its mysticism easier to analyse. The writer dared to offer these new ideas believing that they may be appreciated as the contribution of a scholar towards rendering this old and dying practice in a language that will open it up to the new religious experience of the Igbo.

Pictorial Illustrations

Fig 1: *Ajaezi*

This picture taken by the author (January, 2008) at Ezi-Elias Junction, Enugwu-Ukwu, Anambra State, Nigeria, represents the remains of the commonest form of sacrifice among practitioners of ITR. Items that could be identified in this deposit are:

- A wooden basket (made from palm-frond)
- Dried carcass of a puppy
- Fresh carcass of a lizard
- Fresh palm leaves twisted at the tip
- Some food items
- Plantain stem with premature tubers
- Pieces of black and white cloths
- Some hairs

NB: There are some other materials that could not be identified.

Comment: It is rash to conclude about the concept and content of sacrifice from the mere appreciation of the kind as seen in the picture above. Sacrifices like this are seen at crossroads, junctions, roadsides, river banks and so forth and generally denoted as Aja. This kind of Aja surely is known to the non-initiate. This kind of Aja may have impressed the mind of Arinze and allies. Ịchụaja as a ritual activity is both mystically and philosophically beyond what is seen in the picture. Meanwhile, this sacrifice whose picture appears above may have been offered by a couple in need of a child. Here fruition is represented in the seeding plantain stem; while lizard catches easily the child's eyes. The hairs are most probably from the pubic regions of the couple. The white and black pieces of cloths represent the human and spirit dimension possibly smeared with the semen of the couple. The food items are for the satisfaction of the malicious and capricious spirits. The carcass of the dog is the powerful symbol of initiation of the child into the cult of Dibịa which Agwụ may confirm in future time.

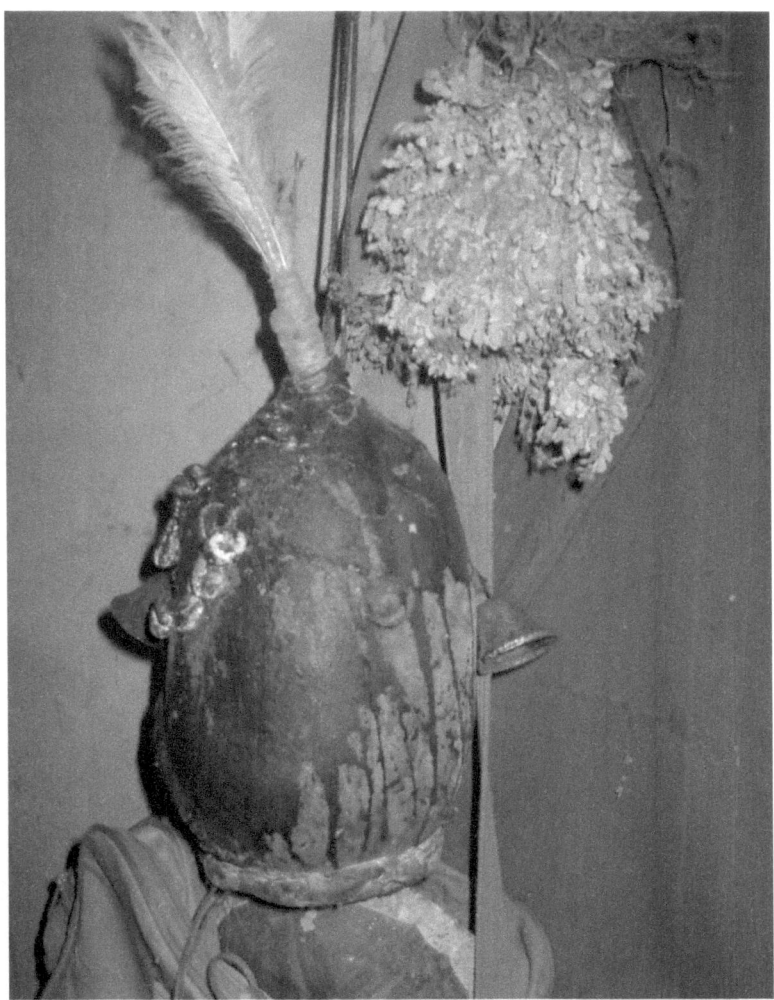

Fig 2: *Anụnụebe*

This is a concoction contained in a calabash and cocked with feathers of the parrot also used in Ituegbo. The Anụnụebe seem to vary from Dibịa to Dibịa not by composition, but in dressing. The stain of blood with which this particular one is periodically energized could be seen which means the exercise of re-energizing was newly done on this. It is said to possess the potency of repelling all kinds of force directed against the bearer.

Comment: The ritual within which many practices in ITR is covered seem to blind the Ofeke – non-initiate to the scientificity of what the Dibịa does. In Ịtụegbo, for instance, the content of this Anụnụebe and the herbs seem to amount to some kind of chemical content which draws energy from the magnetic field of Ala to effect repulsion of like forces directed against it or its bearer who without it would have constituted the other polar region of the energy field attracting this force and causing destructive clashes.

Fig 3: *Ikenga*

This Ikenga belongs to Mr. Edwin Aguoji of Nawfia. This is a gift he received from his father. It may be well over forty years of age. He no longer energizes this Ikenga.

Comment: Ikenga is one of the constituent spirits of Arụsị. It is the symbol of strength for any male especially the Dibia. Before he could perform the ritual of Ịrụagwụ, his Ikenga must take its place, energized to counter all the menacing pranks of Agwụ. So does it evoke his mental/spiritual energy as well as his extrasensory perception during Ịgbaafa. Ikenga reserves the numerological significance of three – strength and readiness for action typified in life itself.

Fig 4: *Akpatiọgwụ*

This is a wooden box containing various shapes and sizes of wood. This box also belonging to Mr. Edwin Aguoji has survived the past forty years and more. Each of the wood represents the various times when and needs in his life for which he consulted the Dibịa. These pieces of woods are symbols to counter external forces or to fortify internally generated ones for the bearer. They get their own portion when sacrifices aimed at energizing them are offered; most times they are smeared with blood of victims. The most prominent of the woods in this box is the Ọfọ (Detarium Senegalese/Elastica). The rest includes Nzu (white chalk), Ọja (flute) and Uhie (Pancake from acacia wood).

Comment: Care must be taken not to understand these pieces of wood as kinds of gods; nor are they nonsensical. The Igbo are deep in symbolisms and their mystical connotations and effects. Imitative arts were not very specialized in the Igbo world and not all Dibịa are artists of sorts. Incapacitated as such, they cannot dash the indispensability of symbols. These pieces of woods may not be particularly attractive to the eyes but they carry the weight of the enormous life reality they represent for the votary. Without Ọfọ, none of the Ọgwụ can work; without being upright there will be no contact between the energies of Ọfọ and any of the Ọgwụ.

REFERENCES

Abasika, E. T. M. (1993). *The conspiracy and the world's best kept secret*. Ibadan, Nigeria: Intes.

Arazu, R. C. (1994). *Covenant broken and reconciliation*. Enugu, Nigeria: Liz Press.

Arazu, R. C. (2003). *Man know thyself*. Enugu, Nigeria: SNAAP Press.

Arazu, R. C. (2005). *Our religion—Past and present*. Awka, Nigeria: Martin-king Press.

Arinze, F. A. (1970). *Sacrifice in Ibo religion*. Ibadan, Nigeria: Ibadan University Press.

Awolalu, J. O., & Dopamu, P. A. (1979) *West African traditional religion*. Ibadan, Nigeria: Onibonoje Press.

Basden, G. T. (1966). *Niger Ibos*. London: Frank Cass.

Batto, B. (1999) Myth. In J. A. Komonchak, M. Collins, & D. A. Lane (Eds), *The new dictionary of theology* (pp. 697-701). Bangalore: Theologica Publications in India.

Catechism of the Catholic Church. (1992). Ibadan, Nigeria: Intec.

Charpentier, E. (1981). *How to read the Old Testament*. Bombay: St Paul's.

Clifford, R. J., & Murphy, R. E. (1995) Genesis. In R. E. Brown, J. A. Fitzmyer, & R. E. Murphy (Eds), *The new Jerome biblical commentary*. Bangalore: Theological Publications in India.

Daly, R. J. (1999) Sacrifice. In J. A. Komonchak, M. Collins, & D. A. Lane (Eds.), *The new dictionary of theology* (pp. 923-925). Bangalore: Theological Publications in India.

De Vaux, R. (1961). *Ancient Israel: Its life and institutions*. London: Darton, Longman, and Todd.

Dumbrell, W. J. (1992). *The faith of Israel*. Leicester, England: Apollos.

Ejiofor, L. U. (1981). *Dynamics of Igbo democracy*. Ibadan, Nigeria: Oxford University Press.

Ejizu, C. I. (1992). Cosmological perspective on exorcism and prayer-healing in contemporary Nigeria. In C. U. Manus, L. N. Mbefo, & E. E. Uzukwu (Eds.), *Healing and exorcism: The Nigerian experience* (pp. 11-23). Enugu, Nigeria: SNAAP Press.

Ekwunife, A. N. O. (1990). *Consecration in Igbo traditional religion*. Enugu, Nigeria: SNAAP Press.

Ekwunife, A. N. O. (1999). *Meaning and function of "ino uwa" in Igbo traditional religious culture*. Onitsha, Nigeria: Spiritan.

Ekwunife, A. N. O. (n. d.). *Introducing African Traditional Religion*. Lecture Note, University of Nigeria Nsukka.

Frazer, G. J. (1976). *The Golden Bough* (abridged edition). London.

Hauret, C. (1973). Sacrifice. In Leon-Dofour, X. (Ed.), *Dictionary of biblical theology* (pp. 512-515). Dublin: Geoffrey and Chapman.

Holy Bible (RSV). (1991). In *The complete parallel Bible*. New York: Oxford University Press.

Idowu, E. B. (1973). *African traditional religion*. London: SCM Press.

Ifesie, E. I. (1989). *Religion at the grassroots*. Enugu, Nigeria: SNAAP Press.

Koch, R. (1969). Vers Une Morale De L'Alliance. In R. Arazu (Ed.), *Covenant Broken And Reconciliation*. Enugu, Nigeria: Liz Press. (Reprinted from *Studia Moralia, 6*, 1969)

Leonard, A. G. (1968). *The lower Niger and its tribes*. London: Frank Cass.

Madu, J. E. (2004). *Honest to African cultural heritage*. Onitsha, Nigeria: Coskan.

McGrath, B., & Imschoot, P. (1963). Sacrifice. In L.F. Hartman (Trans.), *Encyclopedic dictionary of the Bible*. Turnhout, Belgium: Usines Brepols S. A.

Mauss, M. (1954). *The Gift*. London:Routeledge and Kegan Paul

Mbiti, J. S. (1975). *African religions and philosophy*. London: Heinemann.

Metuh, E. I. (1981) *God and man in African religion*. Enugu, Nigeria: SNAAP Press.

Metuh, E. I. (1985*). African religions in Western conceptual schemes*. Jos, Nigeria: IMICO Press.

Metuh, E. I. (1987). *Comparative studies of African traditional religion*. Jos, Nigeria: IMICO Press.

Murphet, H. (1967). —God died? In F. Tanner (Ed.), *The mystery teachings in world religions*. Wheaton, IL: Theosophical.

Njoku, F. O. C. (2002). *Essays in African philosophy, thought and theology*. Enugu, Nigeria: SNAAP Press.

Nwosu, J. A. & Otteh, E. (Rev. & Ed.). *Katikizim nke okwukwe nzuko Katolik n'asusu Igbo*. Onitsha, Nigeria: Excel Publishers.

Ogbukagu, I. N. (1997). *Traditional Igbo beliefs and practices*. Owerri, Nigeria: Novelty Industrial.

Ogbukagu, I. N. (2001). *The Igbo and the riddles of their Jewish origins*. Enugu, Nigeria: Okike.

Ogunmodede, F. (2001). *Of history and historiography in African philosophy*. Ibadan, Nigeria: Hope.

Prabhupada, A. C. B. S. (1984). *Bhagavad-Gita as it is*. Mumbai, India: Bhaktivedanta Book Trust.

Prabhupada, A. C. B. S. (1999). *Beyond illusion and doubt*. Mumbai, India: Bhaktivedanta Book Trust.

Rattray, S. (1985). Worship. In P. J. Achtemeier, R. S. Boraas, M. Fishbane, P. Perkins, & W. O. Walker (Eds.), *Harper's Bible dictionary*. Bangalore: Theological Publications in India.

Sacrosanctum Concilium (The constitution on the sacred liturgy). (1987). In A. Flannery (Ed.), *Vatican Council II*. Dublin: Dominican.

Suarez, F. (1990). *The sacrifice of the altar*. Lagos, Nigeria: Criterion.

Smith, E. W. (1950). African Ideas of God. London: Edinburgh House Press.

Tylor, E. B. (1971). *Primitive Culture* (Vol. 1&2). London.

Umeh, J. A. (1997-1999). *After God is dibia* (Vols. 1-2). London: Karnak House.

Uzukwu, E. E. (1988). *Religion and African culture*. Enugu, Nigeria: SNAAP Press.

Von Cochem, M. (1996). *The holy sacrifice of the mass explained*. Plumpton, Australia: BAC Australia.

William, C. (1987). *The destruction of Black civilization*. Chicago: Third World Press.

APPENDIX I

List of Interviewees

Name	Age	Area	Location	Status	Date
Onyekesi Okpalansofor (A.K.A. Okpalakubuike)	93 years	Agbelu-Akpo, Aguata L.G.A., Anambra State	North- Central Igbo	Long-Standing Practice in ITR (Over 70 Years)	April 23, 2006.
Mmaduka Okpalaonyido (A.K.A. Omemgbeoji)	82 years	Agbelu-Akpo, Aguata L.G.A., Anambra State	North- Central Igbo	Ardent Votary of ITR from birth	April 24, 2006.
Okafor Okonkwo (A.K.A. Nwatadibia)	67 years	Okwurokwu, Amannachi, Orsu L.G.A., Imo State.	Southern Igbo	Dibịaọgwụ	April 5, 2006
Edwin Aguoji (A.K.A. Otugo)	54 years	Nawfia, Njikoka L.G.A., Anambra State.	North-Central Igbo	Dibịaafa	May 19, 2006

Marcel Ugwu (A.K.A. Onwa)	49 years	Obukpa Nsukka	Northern Igbo	Eye-witness to some ITR practices	March 2, 2006
Rev. Fr. Dr. L.C. Chinagorom	43 Years	Ogwa, Imo State	Inland East Igbo	Scholar in Igbo Language	Intermitent Consultations
Ikechi Olisa (A.K.A. Ndilika)	75 Years	Asaba, Delta State	Western Igbo	Ezemmụọ	May 27, 2006
Dike Ofuluozor	90 Years	Nteje, Oyi L.G.A., Anambra State	North-Western Igbo	Dibịaafa	May 15, 2006
Alphonsus U. Nwosu	82 Years	Akwu-Akokwa, Ideato North L.G.A., Imo State.	South-Central Igbo	Elder Statesman and Christian	May 1, 2006.

APPENDIX II

Excerpts from the Interview
with Onyekesi Okpalansofor

(AKA Okpalakubuike)

Author: *Gịnị bụ Ịchụaja?* (What is *Ịchụaja*?)

Okpalakubuike: *Ịchụaja   bụ   ịkpara   ụmụmmụọ   nni.*
(*Ịchụaja* is a means by which the spirits are fed)

Author: *Gini ka o jiri dị mkpa na a ga-akpara ụmụmmụọ nni?*
(Why is it important that the spirits be fed?)

Okpalakubuike: *Ọọ a chụọ aja ikpe owere ma ndi mmụọ. Ka
ụmụ mmadụ were bikwata n'ụwa, e je na-atụ mmụọ nni.*
(It is when sacrifices are properly offered that the spirits
can be blamed for misfortunes. In order that humans may
conveniently habit the earth, the spirits must be fed)

Author: *Kedụ ụdị mmụọ a na-achụnyere aja?* (To what manner of
spirit may this sacrifice be offered?)

Okpalakubuike: *Mmụọ dị ọtụtụ, onweghi nke anaghi achụnyere
aja. A na-achụrụ ezelu aja, na-achụ nke arụsị dị icheiche. Ndị
gboo di naa aja mọbụ ụmụ ekwensu na agwụ na akalogeli.*

(There are varieties of spirits; there is none which is not qualified to receive sacrifice. It can be offered to the King of the sky; it can be offered to different localized spirits. The ancestors even require sacrifices or even the menacing and capricious spirits of *Ekwensu, Agwụ,* or *Akalogeli*.)

Author: *Gịnị mere aja a na-achụrụ mmụọ jiri dị icheiche?* (Why are sacrifices varied; not uniform?)

Okpalakubuike: *Ọọ afa ma nkee. Ndị be anyị sị 'onye na-achụ aja ọ hụrụ mmụọ?' Kedụ ka mmadụ ga-esi jee ịchụ aja ma ọ bụghị ụzọ jee n'afa? Ọọ afa na-ekwu ihe e ji achụ aja mọbụ mmụọ a ga-achụrụ aja.* (It is *Afa* that knows the answer to that. Our people say "Does he who offer sacrifices see the spirits?" How then can one offer sacrifices without first of all consulting with *Afa*? It belongs to *Afa* to recommend the victim and the spirit-beneficiary of sacrifice.

Author: *Yabụonyeagaghịn'afaagaghịamaihenaetuaga-esichụaja?* (Does this imply that without consulting *Afa*, one may not know what and how to offer (in) sacrifice?

Okpalakubuike: *Kedụ ka ọ ga-esi ma? Aja na-awa awa. Etu onye si a chu aja bu etu aja siri wara ya na'afa.* (How else will one know? The need for *Aja* is revealed. How one performs a sacrifice is in accordance with the manner *Afa* reveals it.)

Author: *Kedu mgbe e jigasi achụ aja?* (At what periods may sacrifice be offered?)

Okpalakubuike: *Nwa m, aja bakwarani aba. Etu ihe si eme na ndu onye ka o si achụ aja. Onye ọ gazirighị, ọ chọba dibịa ka ọ gwa ya nke mee bụ.* (My son, sacrifices are infinitely varied. One does sacrifice in accordance with his life situations. If one's plans are not falling in place, he needs to consult with the diviner, who in turn tells him what to do.)

Author: *Ịchụaja onwere myiri n'ala Igbo?* (What and what in Igbo culture could be similar to *Ịchụaja?*)

Okpalakubuika: *Onweghi ihe yiri ya, kpatara e ji achụ ya kwa mgbe kwa mgbe. Ihe ọbụla onye Igbo ga-eme na-ana aja.* (Nothing could be similar to it, and for this same reason, it is ceaselessly offered. Whatever the Igbo do requires some form of *Ịchụaja.*)

Author: *Nna anyi ukwu biko kọwaa ya ọfụma.* (Could you expand on this, sir?)

Okplalkubuike: *Na nghọta nke anyi, Chukwu nọ anyi nso; ụmụmmụo nọ anyị nso; ndị mbụ na ndị egede nọ anyi nso. Ihe ha apịnyeghị aka na ya anaghị agazị. Aja ka e ji achụke ha. A na-eme Ala mọbụ Nkwọ mọbụ Ogoovu, a na-achụ aja. Ọdachi dị mọbụ ihe afọ nghenghe a na-achụ aja.* (In our understanding, God is near to us; the spirits are near to us; our revered ancestors are near to us. Whatever all these do not endorse may not be a success in human life. With *Aja*, they are energized. When we celebrate *Ala*, *Nkwọ*, or *Ogovu*, we offer sacrifices. If there is calamity or tensed situation, sacrifices are offered)

Author: *Ịchụaja na Ịchụogbunuke obu ofu ihe?* (Is *Ịchụaja* and *Ịchụogbunuke* the same?)

Okpalakubuike: *Mbanị! Ogbunuke na ekwensu na akalogeli bụ nwanne. A nakwa- akụrụ ha nni ma ha see nyebe nsogbu, ọ bụkwa ịchụaja n'otu akụkụ.* (O no! *Ogbunuke*, *Ekwensu*, and *Akalogeli* are related. They also are fed when they menace people. On the one hand, that is sacrifice.)

Author: *A na-achụrụ Chukwu aja?* (Are sacrifices offered to *Chukwu?*)

Okpalakubuike: *Ọọ Obinigwe, Ezeiheanyịghị? Eeyini! Ịchụaja bụ otu o siri wa ka e si achụ ya. Afa naa ajaezelu, a ga-achụ ya. Ezelu bu Obingwe, Ezeanyanwụ, osebuluwa....*

199

(Do you mean "He who lives in the skies above; Adept of impossible feats?" O yes! You do sacrifices in accordance with the revelations of *Afa*. If *Afa* recommends a sacrifice for the King of Heaven, so shall it be. The King of Heaven is He was dwells in the skies above, who reigns in the sun, the bearer of the world....)

Author: *E nwere ike iji nnukwu ihe di ka ehi chụ aja?* (Can big things like cow be used for *Ịchụaja*?)

Okpalakubuike: *Ihiei, nwa m abụdị m afa? Afa naa mmadu a na-enye. Ọọ ihe waranị ka e ji achụ. O nwere ike ibụ ihe ọbụla.* (Oo gosh! My son, am I *Afa*? If *Afa* demands as much as a human being, it shall be given. It is that which is revealed that is sacrificed. It may be anything.)

Author: *E nwere ike isi na ịchụaja bụ ịchụpụ ajọ ihe?* (Can we then say that *Ịchụaja* is same as driving away evil?)

Okpalakubuike: *Ọọ ihe ọ bụ! A chụọ aja a chụọ ajọ ihe, ma aja abụghị ajọ ihe. Ọbụbọ juru ụwa, aja na-achụ ọbụbọ.* (Surely that is the implication. When sacrifices are offered, calamities are averted; it should, however, be noted that *Aja* is not evil. The world is rife with precarious situations, *Aja* affords one of stability.)

Comment

We decided to record this interview in the original language, lest we lose the finesse of it. The contents therein have already been discussed in the work. In his last statement as above, Okpalakubuike made a very subtle distinction between *aja* and *ajọ ihe*. He insinuated that the consequence of *Ịchụaja* is the cessation of *ajọ ihe*, yet *aja* itself is not *ajọ ihe*. This is important in the idea of "pursuing evil," which we have dealt with. It cannot be implied that *Ịchụaja* is "pursuing evil" except that by *is* is meant 'consequence.'

Index

B

Bible 30, 32, 48, 93, 152, 193, 194
Brahman 44
Buddhism xxv, 7, 40, 44

C

Candra 42
Catholics 52, 53, 54, 164
Catholic Church xii, xxiii, 49, 51, 53,
    54, 108, 164, 191
cCommunion 63
Chi 20, 23, 68, 140, 169
Christ xiii, 48, 49, 50, 51, 52, 53, 54,
    58, 76, 80, 108, 110, 128, 145,
    164, 176, 180
Christianity xxv, xxvi, xxxi, xxxiv,
    7, 9, 11, 12, 48, 49, 50, 52, 54,
    57, 58, 61, 76, 78, 79, 108, 110,
    127, 128, 151, 173, 176, 177,
    180, 182
Chukwu xxv, xxix, 23, 84, 93, 94, 95,
    98, 99, 104, 118, 138, 151, 152,
    154, 175, 199
communion xiii, 13, 17, 18, 33, 63,
    69, 75, 77, 92, 93, 98, 111, 119,
    127, 129, 148, 164, 167
conjuration 64, 65, 122
cross, the 52
cross, thethe cross 51, 52, 54

D

Darwin 9
Dibia 24, 140
disembodied spirits xxvi, 99, 148

E

Edo xxviii, 146
Efik xxviii
Efikdonaelis 4
Emekọta 19
Eucharist 52, 53, 54, 75
    Eucharistic 52, 53, 54, 164
evil spirits xxviii, 16, 17, 59, 62, 64,
    81, 99, 128, 129, 175
expiation xiii, 8, 58, 64, 65
Ezechitokeabjama xxv
Ezeimo 70
Ezekoro 70, 78

H

hatta'th 37
hHolocaust 63
Hinduism xxv, 7, 40, 177
holocaust 32, 38, 77
Holy of Holies 39, 52
Holy Spirit 147
Holy Spirit, the 49

I

Ibibio xxviii, 3
Idoma xxviii
Ife-nta 4
Ifenru 58, 72
Igala xxviii
Igbaamaonwe 58
Igbo Traditional Religion. See ITR
Igbuaja 58, 82, 114, 123
Ihunru 58, 72, 73, 75, 113, 117
Ijaw xxviii
Ikpuọbụbọ 168
Imedommụọ xxxiv, 64, 65, 66, 75, 78,
    118, 124, 148
immolation 15, 17, 31, 47, 75, 77, 80,
    83, 84, 108, 114, 119, 126, 147,
    148, 152, 179, 180
Indra 42
Irummụọ xxxiv, 118, 119, 124
Irunru 58, 72, 113, 147
ITR xxiii, xxv, xxvi, xxvii, xxx, xxxii,
    xxxiv, xxxv, 4, 5, 6, 7, 11, 12,
    16, 17, 20, 22, 57, 58, 59, 61,
    62, 63, 64, 65, 66, 69, 75, 77,
    78, 80, 100, 103, 107, 110, 111,
    112, 114, 115, 117, 124, 127,
    128, 133, 145, 147, 148, 151,
    152, 155, 159, 160, 161, 166,
    167, 170, 174, 175, 177, 178,
    179, 180, 181, 182, 183, 184,

195, 196
Itualụsọ 58

J

Jesus Christ xxx, 48, 49, 50, 54
Jew xxx, 3, 6, 14, 77, 103, 169, 183
Jewish xxviii, 5, 27, 29, 30, 48, 95,
    100, 103, 151, 176, 194
Judaism xxxi, 7, 27, 28, 30, 31, 36,
    48, 50, 53, 54, 63, 76, 77, 108,
    180, 182

K

Kalabari xxviii, 3
Krishna 40, 42, 43, 45, 46

L

Last Supper 51, 53, 54, 180
localized spirits xxvi, 198

M

Mass xxx, 52, 74
Mayavadi 41
Mbembe xxviii

N

Ndịichie xxvi, 117
Nguma 71
nNru 72
Nri 92, 93, 94, 95, 148, 151, 152
nru 74

O

Obinigwe xxv, 66, 93, 98, 99, 117,
    148, 174, 178, 199
oblation 15, 17, 75, 108, 119, 126,
    137, 141, 149, 180
Ogoni xxviii
Okike 23
Okorie 4
Olah 31, 32, 63, 77
Olisa xxv, 152, 196
original sin 48, 49, 50

Osebulụwa xxv, 148
Osu (Amosu) 19

P

polytheism 7, 9
Protestants 51
pure spirits xxvi, 97, 148

S

sacrifice x, xi, xii, xiii, xxvi, xxvii,
    xxviii, xxxii, xxxiii, 7, 13, 14,
    15, 16, 17, 18, 20, 22, 23, 27,
    29, 30, 31, 32, 33, 34, 35, 36,
    37, 38, 39, 40, 43, 44, 45, 46,
    47, 50, 51, 52, 53, 54, 57, 58,
    59, 60, 62, 63, 65, 66, 69, 71,
    74, 76, 77, 78, 79, 81, 82, 83,
    84, 95, 108, 109, 110, 111, 114,
    119, 126, 127, 128, 134, 135,
    136, 137, 140, 141, 142, 143,
    144, 151, 152, 153, 154, 155,
    156, 160, 161, 164, 168, 170,
    175, 177, 178, 180, 183, 184,
    194, 197, 198, 199, 200
selamim 33, 34, 35
Shechenigbo 4
spirits
  disembodied xxvi, 99, 148
  evil xxviii, 16, 17, 59, 62, 64, 81,
    99, 128, 129, 175
  localized xxvi, 198
  pure xxvi, 97, 148

T

theistic xxv
Tiv xxviii

U

Urhobo xxviii

V

Varuna 42
Vedas 40, 41, 43, 45, 46, 47

Vedic 4, 5, 6, 7, 10, 40, 41, 42, 43, 44,
        45, 47, 54, 108, 127, 161, 180
Vishnu 45
votary xxxiv, 11, 36, 43, 44, 45, 47,
        63, 100, 127, 128, 160, 167,
        171

Y

Yako xxviii

Z

Zebah Selamim 31, 33, 34

www.ingramcontent.com/pod-product-compliance
Lightning Source LLC
Chambersburg PA
CBHW030304290526
45785CB00001B/205